ESTHER: FOR SU

The *Character and Charisma* series introduces us to people in the Bible and shows how their lives have much to teach us today. All the authors in the series use their communication skills to lead us through the biblical record and apply its encouragements and challenges to our lives today. Every volume contains an *Index of Life Issues* to enhance its usefulness in reference and application.

Other books in the series:

CHARACTER AND CHARISMA SERIES

Esther
For Such a Time as This

JILL HUDSON

KINGSWAY PUBLICATIONS
EASTBOURNE

Unless otherwise indicated, biblical quotations are
from the New International Version © 1973, 1978, 1984
by the International Bible Society.

Verses marked AV = Authorised Version, Crown copyright.
GNB = Good News Bible © American Bible Society 1976,
published by the Bible Society and HarperCollins.

ISBN 0 85476 860 2

Published by
KINGSWAY PUBLICATIONS
Lottbridge Drove, Eastbourne, BN23 6NT, England.
E-mail: books@kingsway.co.uk

Designed and produced for the publishers by
Bookprint Creative Services, P.O. Box 827, BN21 3YJ, England.
Printed in Great Britain.

Contents

Timeline

All dates are BC

539	King Cyrus (Kurash) of Persia allows the Jews within his empire to return home from exile
521	King Darius (Daryavaush) ascends the Persian throne
516	The restoration of the Jerusalem Temple is completed
c. 495	Birth of Esther (Hadassah)
486	Death of Darius
486	Xerxes (Kshayarsha/Ahasuerus) ascends the Persian throne
483	The king's wife Vashti is discredited
482	Destruction of Babylon by Persia
483–480	Persia prepares for expedition against Greece
480	Persian expedition against Greece
480–479	Xerxes dallies in Sardis
479	Xerxes returns to Shushan. The search for a new queen begins
478	Esther is brought before the king, and subsequently becomes queen
474	Haman draws lots to determine an auspicious day for the Jews' destruction
473	13 Adar – the 'Day of doom' (early spring)
465	Assassination of Xerxes

Note

Of the above dates, those relating to the history of Persia and its kings have been established by classical scholars from inscriptions and from the writings of ancient Greek authors such as Herodotus and Thucydides. Most of those dates concerned specifically with the story of Esther are based on what the biblical author himself tells us, provided that we are right in identifying his Ahasuerus with Herodotus' Xerxes.

In the biblical text, dates are based upon kings' regnal years. Persian regnal years ran from the Persian New Year, in spring, and the first *full* year during which a king occupied the throne counted as his first regnal year. So the first regnal year of Xerxes was spring 485 to spring 484.

Introduction

Have you ever realized that of all the sixty-six books in the Bible, thirty-seven are named after men, but only two after women?

The first of the two is Ruth. Like so many of the women we meet in the pages of Scripture, Ruth is remembered chiefly because she was a mother who had some very important descendants. Touching and romantic though her story may be, I don't suppose that it would ever have come down to us had she not turned out to be the great-grandmother of King David.

But the second, Esther, is different. In common with just a few biblical heroines – Rahab, Deborah and Jael are the most famous – Esther is remembered for something which she herself achieved. In an act of tremendous courage she saved her people, the Jews, from the threat of extinction, as a result of which she has been hailed as a champion of feminism as well as of Judaism. Quite how much of a champion she was at heart, and whether she was any sort of feminist, we'll be exploring when we take a look together at the extraordinary events of her life.

As a historical novelist I adore a good story – and stories don't come much better than Esther's. For in a classic rags-to-riches drama this beautiful orphan girl living obscurely in exile with her devout male cousin becomes queen of the vast empire in which her nation has been swallowed up. Then an arrogant villain, positively oozing with insidious charm, succeeds in twisting her royal husband around his little finger, and Esther's people find themselves facing annihilation. With her marriage and her very life at stake, Esther must attempt the impossible; and the account of how she sets about this, dispatching her enemies into the bargain, is packed with the most delicious irony and suspense.

All in all, the atmosphere of this stirring tale seems to resemble something from *The Arabian Nights* more than a sacred text, and its plot distinctly reminds us of *Cinderella*. Despite the gravity of the threat to the Jews which it recounts, the book has the flavour almost of carnival, taking unashamed pleasure in the sensational nature of its subject matter and in the consummate expertise with which this has been woven into narrative form. The descriptions of palace life are sumptuous and extravagant; brilliant characterization is achieved with a subtle phrase here and a brief snatch of dialogue there, and we who read or listen to the story are kept on the edges of our seats for much of the time as we witness the villain digging a deeper and deeper pit for himself to fall into. Only in the marvellous 'Joseph' sequence in Genesis 37–50 do we find anything remotely parallel in Scripture.

It's just a pity that we have absolutely no idea who the author of 'Esther' was. Some scholars, basing their ideas on Esther 9:29, have suggested that it was Esther herself; others, taking their cue from Esther 9:20, have supposed it was her cousin. (This is the traditional Jewish view.) But we simply don't know, because the text doesn't tell us. From the kind of language the author uses, we can be fairly confident that he or she wrote not so very long after the events described; many of the words used are borrowed from the Persian of the period, whereas there are hardly any words of Greek origin such as are found in later Hebrew and Aramaic. In any case, from here on I shall be referring to the author as 'he', partly because female authors were very much rarer than male ones in the ancient world, and partly for the sake of simplicity.

But what does his exotic period piece have to teach us today? Does it deserve a place in the Bible at all?

Historically, Jews and Christians have reacted to the book of Esther rather differently. Jews tend to prize it highly; Rabbi Simeon ben Lakish (c. AD 300) said it was equal in importance to the Torah (the five books of Moses). Although its acceptance into the Jewish canon was by no means automatic, and no trace of it has been found in the ancient library of Qumran, it is easy to appreciate the book's appeal to a race that has encountered horrendous persecution down through the centuries and has almost always had a struggle to preserve its distinctive identity. The carnival atmosphere of 'Esther' is vividly reflected in the merry Jewish festival of Purim to which it gave rise: children shake football rattles to drown out the villain's name when the scroll is read in the synagogue, and adults are commanded to drink until they can no longer distinguish between cursing the villain and blessing Esther's cousin who is exalted over him! Undoubtedly the Jews' unquenchable zest for life and their ability to find humour in the direst of circumstances have contributed significantly to their survival as a people to this day.

Many Christians, on the other hand, have found the book problematic. Although superficially it is as simple to understand and enjoy as a children's pantomime, lurking beneath its surface are some difficult questions which have made certain of its readers uncomfortable. Martin Luther even said that he wished the book had never been written. For example, how can we be expected to believe that the events described in 'Esther' ever took place, when some of them sound so much like excerpts from a fairy tale? A beauty contest involving all the eligible maidens in the Near and Middle East; a banquet in which a king proclaims: 'Ask of me what you will, even unto half my kingdom'; a lengthy chain of mind-boggling coincidences dependent on key individuals being in exactly the right place at the right time – how can we credit that these things truly happened, especially when there is no independent record of a Jewish girl ever having been married to a Persian king?

Secondly, what are we to make of the shocking bloodbath in which the Jews' enemies are ultimately – and with considerable relish – exterminated? Doesn't Esther emerge from the massacre as a fiend every bit as brutal and bloodthirsty as the villain she has vanquished? Isn't there a danger that the readers of her story may draw the conclusion that 'might is right', and be tempted to resort to violence themselves?

Thirdly, why is the book named after Esther and not after her cousin, since he appears to be the brains behind her success? There doesn't seem to be much emphasis on Esther's faith or piety; on initial acquaintance with her, we might be forgiven for asking whether she is genuinely worthy of a place in a series called 'Character and Charisma'.

Fourthly – and this is the most puzzling question of all – why is God so conspicuous by his absence throughout these weird and wonderful proceedings? Not only does he not appear to do anything or to say anything to any of the characters in the story, but he doesn't get a single mention from start to finish! This peculiar state of affairs so perplexed the writer who first translated 'Esther' from Hebrew into Greek that he decided to do something about it: he presumptuously inserted 50 references to God so that his version would be politically – or rather, religiously – correct. We shall be referring to this Greek version of 'Esther' again in due course. It was composed for inclusion in the Septuagint, the earliest non-Hebrew translation of the whole Jewish Bible, some time in the third or second century BC. It departs from the Hebrew in a number of important respects; some of them we shall be looking at later on, but they can be found all together in the Apocrypha.

The questions we have raised above are certainly challenging, but they *do* all have answers: answers which show us that God inspired the writer of 'Esther' just as surely as he inspired every other author who contributed to the Bible as we have it today. The book of Esther in its original, canonical version, contains lessons for us which are far more challenging than the questions it may cause us to ask, and the character of Esther herself is such that if we take the trouble to get to know her a little better, time spent in her company will be richly rewarded. She was no stained-glass saint, but a flawed human being like the rest of us, who had to find out the hard way who she really was and what God had called her to do. As we watch her responding to her circumstances and finally rising above them, we shall come to understand what the book that bears her name has to say to us, why it *does* bear her name and not her cousin's, and why its place in the Christian scriptures is wholly justified.

First of all, then, let's journey back in time to the city where Esther lived as a child, growing up like Cinderella with neither mother nor father, in another man's house, and in a foreign land.

1

The Cinderella of Shushan

The citadel of Shushan gleamed like a golden coronet adorning the mound on which it was built. So brightly did it shine in the dazzling sunlight, it was as though fires had been lit along the length of its walls. Of the countless weary travellers who wended their way towards it, those who had never before set eyes upon it reined in their horses, put down their burdens, or simply stopped in their tracks to stare.

From all across the vast Persian empire they had come: provincial administrators, each with his entourage of civil servants; military commanders with their highest-ranking officers; and aristocrats of every tribe and town. Between them they wore every kind of costume that could be imagined, from flowing robes to tapered trousers. Some of them had brown skin, some black, some yellow, and they spoke in a babel of different tongues. But every one had come in response to the same royal summons.

For the Great King of Persia had invited every governor, every general and every nobleman from the four corners of his realm, along with those who resided in Shushan his capital, to a banquet the like of which had never been thrown before. He had resolved to exhibit to his most eminent subjects the contents of the imperial treasury, and the opulence of his palace – as if they didn't already know how fabulously, obscenely wealthy their overlord was. Some of those making the journey had been on the road for weeks or even months, so extensive were the king's domains.

Yet now at last their goal was in sight. As they approached their destination, they saw that the walls of the citadel were not on fire after all; rather, they were faced with glazed bricks of vivid colours, that captured the sunlight like jewels.

Indeed, the city was a jewel in its own right, clasped in an exquisite setting. To its north and east the Zagros mountains rose up all misty and blue; glittering canals criss-crossed the plain below like silver serpents, and between the canals stretched cornfields and orchards and plantations of palms. To the west of the city flowed a mighty river, along whose banks grew lilies of every variety and hue, so that the inhabitants of the capital had nicknamed their home the City of Lilies. Poplar and cypress offered shade to the farmers who toiled in the fertile fields, and to a stranger's eye, it appeared that all was perfect peace and prosperity.

* * *

From the king's perspective, it certainly was both peaceful and prosperous. Shushan, otherwise known as Susa, his administrative capital, was perhaps the richest metropolis the ancient world had so far produced, and his empire was undoubtedly among the largest. The author of 'Esther' wants us to appreciate this from the outset, for he begins his book not by introducing us to Esther – he leaves his personal introductions until later – but by painting for us a truly sumptuous picture of Persian power and luxury. In Esther 1:1–8 he tells us that the Persian king ruled over

127 provinces, and that his palace was bedecked with gold, silver, marble and precious stones.

Nor is all this by any means a fantasy of our author's own making. His evidence is corroborated by archaeology and by other ancient writers. In the fifth century BC, when our story is set, the domains of the King of Persia extended over nearly two million square miles, stretching from the Mediterranean coast of Turkey eastwards into Asia, and south into Africa and what is now Pakistan – and he received lavish tribute from all his subject peoples. Gold and ivory came from Nubia, frankincense from Arabia, horses and chariots and weapons from Lydia and Caria and from distant lands beyond the Caspian Sea. The king's clothing and the hangings in his palace were dyed with Tyrian purple extracted from a rare species of sea-snail; a single pound's weight of this precious dye cost more than a labourer could hope to earn in a year. When we compare the splendour of the Persian king's existence with the simplicity of the lives of the peasants and nomads we meet elsewhere in Scripture, we seem to have entered a different world.

However, in contrast to the life of luxury enjoyed by the king and his court, some of the people over whom he held sway were in desperate need. In the vast majority of ancient societies there was a huge gap between rich and poor, which is why so much of the Old Testament is concerned with eradicating social injustice among the people of God – in this, as in so much else, Israel was meant to be different from her pagan neighbours.

We who live in the Western world today are frequently being reminded that in comparison with most of the earth's population we are *all* stupendously rich – though we may not feel it, when we recall that Bill Gates has been able to donate 60 million pounds towards vaccinating children in the developing nations against disease! Recently a Christian

friend of mine was privileged to meet a black clergyman
from South Africa who was visiting her parish in order to
find out what British churches were doing for the poor.
Naturally he wanted to meet some underprivileged people
for himself, so that he could talk with them about their
problems and about how the church was trying to help. My
friend took him to a housing estate which is reckoned to be
one of the most deprived in Britain. Having looked around
at the houses, all of which had glass in the windows, and
having learned that all the residents had access to doctors
and schools and clean water and refuse collections, he
asked, 'But where are the homes of the *poor*?'

Of course, poverty and wealth are always relative, and
there is poverty of aspiration as well as material poverty and
indeed poverty of spirit. But the fact is that we in the West
– all of us – are comparatively well off, and to many of our
brothers and sisters in other parts of the world, the lifestyles
of most Western Christians would seem as profligate as that
of the Persian king. By the same token, the King of Persia
would probably have considered Bill Gates' fortune as
being of little account.

However, if we are talking about *relative* wealth, even
ordinary native Persians were better off than most of their
contemporaries. Because of the heavy tribute demanded
from subject nations, Persians themselves did not have to
pay any taxes at all.

But Shushan wasn't populated exclusively by Persians. It
was a thoroughly multicultural society, mostly as a result of
the policies of the Babylonians whose empire Persia had
taken over. The Babylonians, in common with the Assyrians
before them, had been accustomed to skimming off the
cream from the peoples they conquered and carrying away
the noble and the clever into exile to prevent them foment-
ing rebellion. When Jerusalem had fallen to the troops of

Nebuchadnezzar in 587 BC, ancestors of Esther's cousin Mordecai had been among those taken (Esther 2:6), and this was how Mordecai and Esther had come to be living over 600 miles from the land of their fathers.

Not that we know very much at all about Esther and Mordecai's particular circumstances at the beginning of their story. The author of 'Esther' doesn't actually introduce either of them to us until his second chapter, preferring to focus instead on events at court while keeping us guessing as to the role his heroine is going to play in this colourful costume drama. The Greek historian Herodotus, from whom most of our information on ancient Persia derives, tells us nothing about the Jewish community that existed in its capital city. Neither can archaeologists offer us any assistance in this respect – though their excavations have closely corroborated our author's description of the royal palace. The throne room, harem and gardens have all been found and identified, and some of the building materials did indeed come from as far afield as India and Ethiopia (Cush) which Esther 1:1 defines as the limits of the empire.

Did the Jews live all together in a 'ghetto', keeping themselves to themselves, or were they dispersed all over the city? We don't know, but it's very likely that some of them at least mixed quite freely with the Gentile population. For difficult as things may have been for many of them economically, never under Persian rule had they been the victims of persecution. The Persian kings had acquired quite a reputation for tolerance, in contrast to the Assyrians and Babylonians whose empires they had inherited. In fact, this was probably the secret of their success. According to author Brian Dicks, 'the speed and the facility with which the Persian Empire was created are largely explained by the youthful energy of the new conquerors and the revolutionary policy of laissez-faire that meant tolerance, moderation and permissiveness hitherto unknown in the Ancient World'.[1] The Assyrians and Babylonians had repressed conquered nations savagely, destroying religious and social institutions, and enslaving or deporting tens of thousands of people. The Persians, on the other hand, respected the traditions and customs of their subjects.

Cyrus (in Persian 'Kurash'), the founder of the ruling Achaemenid dynasty, had in 539 BC given express permission for peoples whom the Babylonians had taken into exile to return home and rebuild what had been demolished. Cyrus' generous offer is celebrated at the end of 2 Chronicles (2 Chronicles 36:22–23) and in the opening of the book of Ezra (Ezra 1:1–4, 7); the biblical evidence for his action is endorsed by the so-called 'Cyrus cylinder'. This is a clay barrel inscription discovered at Babylon towards the end of the nineteenth century, on which Cyrus himself tells of how captive populations were allowed to return to their own countries and build sanctuaries to their own gods.

However, by no means all of the displaced people within Cyrus' domains had taken him up on his offer, and this was just as true of the Jews as it was of any other ethnic group. It was curiously similar to the situation we find among the Jews in our own time, and similar attitudes must have prevailed then as now. Since the foundation of the modern Israeli state in 1948, many of those Jews who have gone to live there ('made aliyah', as it is called) have earned the frank admiration of many of those who have not. Perhaps some of those Jews who remained in Persia in Esther's day sent money to their brethren in Israel to assist with its reconstruction, just as many American Jews do today.

---

1. Brian Dicks, *The Ancient Persians: How They Lived and Worked* (David & Charles, 1979).

For in the half-century that had elapsed between the fall of Jerusalem and the issuing of Cyrus' edict, many firm roots must have been put down by the exiles in Shushan and its environs. Many of the displaced Jews had worked extremely hard, as they have had to do throughout much of their history, and had pulled themselves up by their bootstraps. Businesses had been established, land had been acquired and farmed, and two generations had grown up to whom Jerusalem and Judah must have meant little more than Pakistan or India mean to some Asians born and bred in Britain. No doubt there had been intermarriage among the minority peoples and with the native Shushanite population, and we can readily understand the reluctance of many to exchange the life they knew for one of uncertainty and probable hardship. By the time of Esther's birth the Jerusalem Temple had been rebuilt (the account of its restoration and the opposition met by those who had under-taken the work can be read in 'Ezra'), but there were no city walls, and many of the houses still lay in ruins. If the Jewish residents of Shushan when Esther was living there as a child constituted a community in crisis, this was a crisis of compromise and assimilation rather than of victimization.

Similarly, in modern times, the Board of Deputies of British Jews has expressed profound concern for the long-term survival of the Jewish community in Britain — not because Jews are still occasionally the target of racist abuse, but precisely because the overwhelming majority of them never are. Most are so well integrated into British society that large numbers of them are 'marrying out' and their children are being brought up with scant regard for their special heritage. It's not easy to decide which has posed the greater threat to the Jews as a people in our own century: assimilation or persecution. Hitler killed six million, yet many of those who survived the holocaust emerged with a stronger sense of identity than they had possessed before. Now this identity is slowly but surely being eroded.

As Christians living in a secular society, our situation is the same, only in some ways worse! We know that we are supposed to be different from those around us, that our lives as well as our words are meant to bear witness to our beliefs. Yet we *don't* belong to a separate ethnic group, and our difference is meant to be such that others are attracted by it rather than finding it strange or threatening. Maintaining our distinctiveness, being salt and light to our neighbours and sharing with them our experience of God without ramming religion down their throats, is a pretty tall order. I for one often feel as though I'm walking a very slippery tightrope from which I plummet to one side or the other with monotonous regularity, by saying either too little or too much. There's nothing I enjoy more than a lively discussion about faith in God with folk who aren't regular churchgoers, but sometimes I'm reluctant to raise the subject – not because I'm afraid of being mocked, but just the opposite. In middle-class European society we're far more likely to encounter polite indifference than anything else. Living respectably and demonstrating a modicum of compassion for those in need is simply not enough – even in our godless era many non-Christians exhibit these characteristics.

At the beginning of his letter to the Ephesians the Apostle Paul explains exactly how we ought to be different, and prays that this difference may become real in the lives of those to whom he is writing. He says:

> I keep asking that the God of our Lord Jesus Christ, the glorious Father, may give you the Spirit of wisdom and revelation, so that you may know him better. I pray also that the eyes of your heart may be enlightened in order that you

may know the hope to which he has called you, the riches of his glorious inheritance in the saints, and his incomparably great power for us who believe. (Ephesians 1:17–19)

In other words, the vital thing is that we get to know God better. If we do, we'll be absolutely certain of what we believe and how incredibly exciting it is, and we'll have direct access to his power. Those who meet us will see God's Spirit shining out of us.

At least, they will unless the eyes of *their* hearts have been blinded entirely by the cares of this world. When I'm not writing my novels I teach part time and am involved in running a youth gospel choir, and sometimes it seems to me that unless God gets through to us during our teenage years it's too late for many of us. As a rule I find teenagers much more ready than adults to talk about things that really matter, and to search for meaning rather than filling up their lives and blocking out their deepest questions with work or trivialities.

What then can we say about Mordecai and Esther themselves in this context? Why were they still living in Shushan when they could have gone back to Jerusalem to play their part in the rebuilding of their nation? Was Mordecai as comfortable and compromised as many of his peers must have been?

Certainly it's unlikely that Mordecai's parents were particularly observant Jews. After all, the name they gave him is derived from that of Marduk, a god of the Babylonians, among whom they had perhaps been rather too eager to win acceptance. 'Marduka' or 'Mardukaya' seems to have been quite a common name among Babylonians and Persians at the time, and it's startlingly different from the names of Mordecai's ancestors which the author of 'Esther' has recorded for us. (A certain Marduka is named in a Persian text from roughly this period as having been an accountant who served on an official tour of inspection launched from Shushan. Could this man and our Mordecai have been one and the same?!)

The truth is that we simply don't know what reasons Mordecai himself might have had for remaining in the Persian capital. However, judging by the way he behaves further on in the book of Esther, refusing to budge so much as an inch from his principles regardless of the consequences, it seems to me highly unlikely that comfort or compromise accounts for his having stayed put in the land to which his forefathers had been banished.

So was he simply a rebel reacting against his parents' moral turpitude, or had he genuinely arrived at a personal faith in God and found his true destiny? Perhaps he was well aware of the subtle dangers to which the Jews of Shushan were exposed, and believed that his ministry lay in remaining among them in order to save them from themselves. Perhaps he ran Torah classes for his Jewish neighbours' sons, striving to awaken in them a sense of their own identity as members of God's chosen people, and to school them in Hebrew, the language of their scriptures, when their natural inclination was to slip into the Aramaic which was spoken by their Gentile playmates.

Then again, it's possible that, like some ultra-Orthodox Jews of today, Mordecai didn't altogether approve of the reconstituted Jewish state, believing that there could be no Israelite kingdom without a legitimate king, and no Temple without the Ark of the Covenant inside it. The Ark had disappeared before or during the war with Babylon, and its whereabouts remains as fascinating a mystery today as has ever existed. As for a king, many of the Jews who had gone back home had pinned quasi-messianic hopes upon one Zerubbabel, who had been appointed governor of Judah by

Cyrus and was of the Davidic line. But although Zerubbabel has been accorded a place of high honour in Jewish tradition because of his close association with the rebuilding of the Temple, there was no way in which he could have won independence from his Persian overlords.

Another factor in Mordecai's thinking may have been the message of prophets like Jeremiah. It was Jeremiah who had received the revelation that the practice of true religion is not dependent on buildings or rituals – in fact, these things can positively get in the way. Genuine spirituality has much more to do with what we are on the inside, than with the forms of worship in which we engage. It is the product of a living relationship with our Creator; Jeremiah called this the 'circumcision of the heart'. Perhaps Mordecai had remained in Shushan because he feared a return to the old ways, to externals, to a denial of the true knowledge of God. The book of Malachi, which is contemporary with the events of 'Esther' but set in Jerusalem, betrays a disillusionment with the restoration. It condemns slovenly practices, insincerity in worship, and a lack of genuine faith among some of those people who had gone back.

What then of little Esther? How had she lost her parents and wound up living with her virtuous and venerable cousin in an alien land? All we are told about her immediate family is her father's name, Abihail. It may be that he and his wife *had* in fact gone back to Jerusalem, where they had thrown themselves with gusto into rebuilding what the Babylonians had torn down. What better reason could they have had for naming their daughter 'Hadassah', which means 'myrtle'? The prophet Zechariah had seen a vision of an angel in a grove of myrtle trees, who had proclaimed God's undying love for his holy city and promised its restitution (Zechariah 1:7–17). The myrtle is also a symbol of peace, joy and life. Isaiah had written that God would plant myrtle trees in the wilderness and cause them to blossom once again. Our heroine probably didn't actually acquire her more familiar name 'Esther' until she was at the palace being prepared for marriage to the Persian king, or at least on the point of going there. This name is related to that of Ishtar, the Assyrian and Babylonian goddess of love and war – which was to turn out to be singularly apposite!

But the life of the pioneers effecting the restoration was probably, as we have said, one of hardship. In the book of Joel, for example, we are told of an appalling plague of locusts which occurred just before Esther's story begins. It was also a life of wretched struggle against the opposition of men who objected to what the pioneers were labouring to achieve. Jews who had never been in exile, those whom the Babylonians had considered too feckless to be worth the effort of deporting (the prophet Jeremiah had called them the 'bad figs' whom God had rejected), together with the Samaritans, who had never belonged to God's people in the first place, took offence at the attitude of those who had returned, because it seemed that they wanted things all their own way. Violent attacks were made upon the builders; possibly it was in one such attack that Esther's parents, along with any brothers and sisters she may have had, lost their lives. (Esther 4:14 implies that Esther was the last of her line.) With Mordecai being her closest surviving relative, she was packed off back to Shushan to be adopted as his daughter.

We are told nothing to suggest that Mordecai had a wife or children of his own. Perhaps they had died too, or else he had never married. Either way, he cannot have found it easy to bring up a bereaved child on his own, nor can she have had an easy ride adjusting to life in his house. Perhaps love grew up between them in the way that it did between Heidi and the Alm Uncle in Johanna Spyri's children's classic. (*Heidi* is another well-loved story with which 'Esther' has more than a little in common.)

Or perhaps it did not. We are told only that Esther 'was obedient to' her adoptive father, but whether she obeyed him willingly or begrudgingly we have no means of telling! It's very probable that she may have been something of a handful as she approached marriageable age; the Bible says that she was uncommonly beautiful (Esther 2:7), and throughout the book that bears her name we cannot fail to notice that she charms every person she meets. Ensuring that her reputation remained intact may well have caused her cousin a few sleepless nights.

It's often imagined that strikingly beautiful people have much easier lives than those of us who were further back in the queue when good looks were being distributed! They have more confidence in themselves, and therefore more friends than anybody else; *everyone* seems to want to know them.

Yet these things are not necessarily advantages in the long run. Popular people are often tempted to rely on themselves or on a wide circle of friends rather than on God. They may become arrogant, and even suppose that everything will always be brought to them on a plate. Also, it can be harder for a person who is popular to risk making a stand for God than for someone who is already experiencing problems with acceptance. As a teenager I frequently had days when I felt like a fish out of water. To find unconditional acceptance for the first time when I joined the school Christian Union was so exciting that I didn't much care what the rest of the school thought of us. My brasher and more gregarious classmates, on the other hand, the ones with big hair, and legs that went up to their armpits, were not about to jeopardize their street cred by 'getting religion'. Somehow I can't help thinking that as pretty little Esther grew up, she might have been rather more like them than she was like me. Influenced as much by her Gentile peers as she was by Mordecai himself, it's highly likely that she would have found the elegant city chic of Shushan society irresistibly attractive.

Whatever the nature of Esther and Mordecai's relationship, all we can say about Esther's role in the early chapters of her book is that it is essentially a passive one. She does as Mordecai tells her; and even if she did rebel against his authority from time to time, as I imagine she did, rebellion is as much a knee-jerk reaction as subservience is. We learn nothing about Esther the child, or even the adolescent first introduced to palace life, that would cause us to suppose there was anything potentially heroic about her.

But this is one of the wonderful things about the narrative sections of the Bible, and of the Old Testament in particular. The skeleton of a storyline is all that Scripture gives us nine times out of ten. Its authors rarely even pass judgement on whether the actions of their characters are right or wrong. For this reason some modern readers tend to find biblical narrative rather disconcerting – codes of law and blatant calls to repentance are so much easier to interpret! The Old Testament supplies tantalizingly little detail about its protagonists' psychological motivation, so that on a superficial reading they sometimes seem to do inexplicable things or act 'out of character' in so far as we feel that we have got to know them.

But in fact this is never the case. We need to remember that the first readers of 'Esther', just like those of the other biblical books, belonged to the same culture as the author and would be able quite easily to 'read between the lines', readily understanding where the characters were coming from. We on the other hand have to work a little harder. On closer inspection we discover that if characters' personalities seem to change during the course of the action, there is always a reason.

And there is no denying that Esther changes a great deal. If as a child and an adolescent she was very much the puppet of the men in her life, this is scarcely surprising considering the culture in which she lived. Yet when subsequently she emerges as an initiator in her own right, the transformation is by no means inexplicable, as we shall see.

2

Meet Prince Charming!

Standing on his private balcony enjoying its spectacular view over the palace gardens, Ahasuerus looked forward with relish to the banquet which he and his advisors had long been planning. For many months countless minions had been drafting invitations and going through replies, making arrangements for the accommodation of literally hundreds of dignitaries, requisitioning and receiving consignments of salt and spices and all kinds of delicacies of the finest quality for his guests' delectation.

The king could no longer recall exactly which member of his Privy Council had first given voice to the idea; in any case, he knew that they invariably phrased their suggestions in such a way as to enable him to believe that he had thought of them himself.

But he could scarcely resist the temptation to smile as he imagined the awe that would be visibly stamped upon his subjects' faces once they were allowed inside the gates of his royal precincts. How they would marvel at the plethora of gold and silver treasures which were at this very moment being readied for display – and they would marvel all the more when they learned that every exquisite item had been brought to the palace as a gift or in tribute by the scion of some royal house whose kingdom Ahasuerus' predecessors had conquered. How their mouths would water at the sight and smell of the exotic dishes his cooks would prepare for their delight, and how they would exclaim in ecstasy when they tasted the wines from the royal cellars.

Even now the governors, generals and noblemen would be converging on his capital city. And with them would come not only their squires, valets and bodyguards, but their wives and children too. While the men feasted their eyes upon Ahasuerus' material treasures, he was well aware that what their womenfolk would be hoping for was to catch a glimpse of *him*.

For the Persian king was blessed with the kind of looks which made girls and even grown women want to faint into his arms on sight. He was young, tall and proud, with the lean physique of a hunter. He had finely chiselled features and lazy, insolent eyes set in a smooth olive skin. His hair – long, dark and luxuriant – and his flowing beard were immaculately curled and glossy with lacquer. His purple robes were so rich in hue and texture, it seemed that they must have been spun, dyed and woven by angels. Whenever he seated himself upon his kingly throne, every fold of his rosette-studded cape and great wide sleeves looked as though it had been accurately measured and painstakingly arranged in deliberate symmetry. Upon his head he would wear an elaborate stiffened headdress encircled by a purple mitra, which proclaimed him to be the earthly representative of his god Ahura Mazda, and the sole rightful incumbent of the Achaemenid throne.

*   *   *

This, then, was the man whom little Esther was destined to marry, and a handsome specimen he certainly was, if the depictions of him on Persian palace friezes are to be believed. Looks, riches, power – he had everything. In fact if we were to give this exalted personage his title in full, it would include the designation 'King of Babylon and Egypt' as well as King of Persia and Lord of its empire – the relevance of which we shall appreciate in due course.

Not that he was particularly eligible, however. For in Esther chapter 1, when we are first introduced to him, Ahasuerus is already married, and we are told that his wife's name is Vashti.

It's true that the Persian king was permitted by law to have more than one wife at any one time, but it doesn't seem that Ahasuerus had taken advantage of this privilege, or that he had any intention of ever doing so. This was probably because he saw polygamy as a foreign influence, and we know that he disapproved of anything foreign contaminating pure Persian customs. Not that this prevented him from keeping his harem well stocked with concubines, who were legally bound to him just as his wife was, but without a wife's legal rights.

Polygamy of course was never meant to be God's way, nor was the keeping of concubines, though in antiquity many kings – including kings of Israel – practised both. Even David, who in so many other respects was a 'man after God's own heart', had several wives and even more concubines (see 2 Samuel 5:13). The Jewish (and subsequently Christian) ideal of one man and one woman being partners for life was – and is – truly radical. In Genesis chapter 2 we learn that when one man and one woman are united in marriage they become one flesh together, and that this unique marital bond is meant to last for life. But it seems that for some reason the kings of Israel decided that this didn't apply to them! Likewise many ancient societies prized women's chastity highly, while having entirely different standards for their menfolk – this is still the case in some traditional communities today, especially in Asian culture.

So who *was* Ahasuerus? Which of the Achaemenid kings are we talking about? The Greek translator of 'Esther' goes for Artaxerxes – presumably because superficially the two names seem very similar. Some 'liberal' scholars say he was no one at all, a mere fiction, like the whole of the rest of the book!

In fact he was almost certainly Xerxes I, son and successor of Darius I Hytaspes, who ascended the Persian throne in 486 BC. Ahasuerus is the Hebrew equivalent of the Persian name Kshayarsha, and the consonants of this name, Kshyrsh, gave rise to the Greek form Xerxes.

What do we know about this Xerxes from other sources? There are no surviving Persian accounts; only a few tantalizing inscriptions. Esther 10:2 refers to the 'annals of the kings of Media and Persia', and in Esther chapter 6 some royal records are read out to the king. But unfortunately we don't possess them. Who knows, perhaps they will turn up one day in a dusty cave, like the Dead Sea Scrolls – or, more likely, in the private collection of some shady dealer in antiquities.

But in the meantime, our principal source for the Persian empire is Herodotus, who wrote in the fifth century BC, and was thus contemporary with many of the people and events he describes. Being Greek, Herodotus belonged to a people very hostile to Persia. This was the period of the flowering of Athenian democracy, arguably the most glorious period in Greek history – and also of the Persian Wars when the Persians tried to add Greece to their domains. However, Herodotus is not at all vitriolic in the way he writes about Greece's enemies. He is like a modern travel writer, fascinated by alien cultures; there is nothing he loves more than describing the outlandish customs of obscure tribes in far-flung parts of his world. And he is quite prepared to be impressed by some aspects of other men's lifestyles, including that of the Persians.

But other Greeks besides Herodotus saw much that was good about the Persian empire. Cyrus was actually cited by some authors – usually those disillusioned with democracy – as a model ruler. However, it seems that Xerxes was very different from Cyrus, and from Cyrus' successors Cambyses and Darius, in a number of important ways. The most notable difference was his zeal for Ahura-Mazda.

Ahura-Mazda (meaning 'Wise Lord') was and still is the God of the Zoroastrians. Zoroastrianism is a religion which began in Persia, but most of its adherents now live in India, where their Persian origin is reflected in the name 'Parsees' by which they are generally known. Zoroaster, or Zarathustra, the founder of this religion, probably lived in the sixth century BC and may well have known Xerxes' father Darius when the latter was a boy. (It is very likely that Xerxes' mother Atossa was Zoroaster's first convert.)

Ahura-Mazda was an Indo-European god who had been worshipped for centuries, but it was Zoroaster who claimed that he was the *only* god – and an invisible one at that. Zoroaster also formulated a more coherent theology out of the old folk beliefs. He declared that man has free will and that his own conscience will determine his future reward. Ahura-Mazda will judge us all, separating the wise from the unwise, the followers of the Truth from those of the Lie. Those found worthy will proceed across the Bridge of the Separator to the House of Song.

So Zoroastrianism in its earliest and purest form was never pagan in the sense of being idolatrous. There were no statues, temples or sacrifices.

Thus it must have been very tempting for some Jews to conclude that Ahura-Mazda was really just another name for the God whom *they* worshipped. And in a sense they might have been right. In so far as all monotheistic religions seek to honour the one single creating and sustaining force behind the universe, they are all worshipping the same God. But their conceptions of him can be radically different, and indeed incompatible. Some must therefore be 'truer' than others! By this I mean that if there is a God at all, he must have certain characteristics, and to the extent that different religions' descriptions of him match up with these characteristics they can be said to be more, or less, true. Of course, this is a very unfashionable stance to take in our twenty-first-century, post-modernist society, in which every man considers himself the arbiter of his own truth. But for Christians truth is to be sought in God's revelation, and not in the whims of fashion.

Furthermore, to say that all monotheists worship the same God can all too easily lead us to conclude that 'all religions are the same really'. Whereas of course they are not! My husband Keith and I once spent several hours talking with a devout Palestinian Muslim in his tent on the West Bank. We agreed about dozens of issues, far more than we ever usually agree about with anyone (such as the evils of materialism and sexual promiscuity, and the religious ignorance of so many millions of people). But the thing we agreed about more strongly than anything else was that Christianity and Islam are radically different! Inter-faith dialogue is a good thing, if by this we mean learning to understand others' beliefs and ensuring that they come to understand ours. But inter-faith worship is another thing altogether. Religions are *not* the same; they are *not* different paths to the same destination. Some of them don't even agree on what the destination is. For example, whereas most religions derive hope from the concept of life continuing beyond the grave, to a Buddhist the annihilation of the individual at death seems like a blessed relief.

Anyway, Xerxes was certainly an adherent of early Zoro-astrianism in a way that his predecessors had not been. Darius' inscriptions acknowledge the existence of other gods in addition to Ahura-Mazda, while those of Xerxes never do. Xerxes was much less tolerant of foreign religious practices within his domains than Cyrus or Darius had been, as his barbaric treatment of the religious institutions of Egypt and Babylon reveals. When these nations revolted against him, he burned their temples and had statues of their deities hacked into pieces and sold for scrap. Like the Assyrians and Babylonians before him, he reduced whole populations to servitude.

He was also obsessed with the related concept of Aryanism – a term with notoriously powerful associations in recent European history. The word 'Aryan' comes from the Sanskrit *arya*, meaning 'noble'. In origin the Aryans were a nomadic stock-breeding people who settled in Iran and North India in prehistoric times. From their language all the Indo-European languages are descended: Sanskrit, Persian, Greek, Latin, Celtic, Slavonic and Teutonic.

Xerxes' inscriptions show his own belief in the superiority of the Aryan race. A text from Persepolis reads: 'Ahura-Mazda is the Great God who gave us this earth and sky, who made Kshayarsha the King reign over multitudes as Sole Sovereign. I am Kshayarsha the Great King . . . a Persian, son of a Persian, an Aryan of Aryan seed.' Another text reads: 'Among the rebellious nations was one where demons were worshipped. Through Ahura-Mazda's favour I destroyed their sanctuary and in that spot I worshipped the Wise Lord.'

Of course, beliefs of this type can be notoriously danger-ous. In the nineteenth century the term 'Aryan' was used as a synonym for Indo-European, and the idea arose that the

'Aryan race' was responsible for all the progress which mankind had made. The Nordic and Germanic peoples came to be regarded as the purest Aryans. It's easy to see how this gave rise to eugenics, and led ultimately to the Nazi policy of exterminating Jews, gypsies and anyone else the Nazis didn't happen to like.

Such 'fundamentalist' ideas on Xerxes' part seem to me to constitute evidence of gross insecurity. Fundamentalism is a difficult word to define to everyone's satisfaction, but what I mean by it in this context is the assumption that not only are your own beliefs entirely exempt from being questioned in any way but that you have the God-given right to impose them upon others, by whatever means are deemed necessary. It seems to me that fundamentalism of this nature is always a sign of insecurity, including Christian fundamentalism. It is not a sin for a Christian to admit that some of the stories in the Bible are perplexing and may be open to more than one interpretation. Nor is it automatically right for Christians to campaign for their nation's laws to be lifted straight from the Bible. We are the first to protest when Islamic nations seek to impose Quranic law on *their* populations. It is understandable that when we reflect upon the godless society in which we live we may be tempted to believe that slipping standards in the world will lead to the collapse of civilization as we know it, and that non-Christians should be forced into moral straitjackets for their own good. But we should always bear in mind that being dogmatic is not the way to win the world for Christ. It was never said that 'by the purity of their doctrine you shall know them'.

Returning to Xerxes, other evidence too points to the fact that he was very insecure. He was haunted by the ghosts of Cyrus and Darius because he knew that they had been great monarchs who had conquered and subdued many rich lands for Persia, and brilliantly organized the running of the huge empire which resulted. He wanted to equal them, yet did not possess the same strength of character.

When he did embark upon ambitious enterprises, they seem to have been doomed to failure. This is probably why in the end he took refuge in enormous building projects, both at Persepolis, his religious capital, and at Susa too. It's interesting that Saddam Hussein has done the same. He regards himself as a second Nebuchadnezzar, but in personality he may be a lot more like Xerxes. I suppose we can only be grateful that most men intent on making their mark in the world lack sufficient resources to indulge their architectural fantasies by erecting colossal edifices all over the countryside.

I believe that insecurity accounts for many of the seemingly contradictory traits we find in Xerxes' personality, both in Herodotus and the book of Esther: impetuousness combined with excessive dependence on his advisors, cruelty combined with a tendency to depression, and an obsession with his own mortality.

We sometimes think of depression as a curse of modern society, but it has always existed, even if it has gone by other names. Its causes have remained much the same too: existential angst (despair over the apparent futility of life), and a preoccupation with one's own perceived shortcomings (I'm ugly; I'm weird; nobody likes me; think I'll go and eat worms . . .). Frankly, the surest cure for both is a vibrant relationship with God! There is depression which is clinical in origin, arising from imbalances in the chemistry of our brains, but drugs alone help no one find life's true meaning.

Can we see something of *ourselves* in the Persian king, who was so eager to make his mark, to make his life count for something? Are we chasing fame or fortune? It will get us nowhere. Xerxes had fame and fortune already, but it wasn't enough. He had a faith, too, but although as a Zoroastrian he was supposed to believe in life after death, there was no guarantee that he would be found worthy to attain it. There was no assurance in Zoroaster's theology, whereas as Christians we *can* know that we shall live for ever, because we depend on Christ's righteousness, not our own. Our lives automatically count for something, because we know that we are loved and accepted by God.

So much for Xerxes' religion and personality. Now let us turn our attention for a moment or two to his marriage. Who exactly was Xerxes' wife? In Herodotus, Xerxes' wife is Amestris, not Vashti. Some commentators have equated Vashti with Esther, again because of superficial similarity in the sounds of their names. But this cannot be correct, because Amestris' third son, the future Artaxerxes I, was born in 483 BC, before Esther was even married according to the dating in 'Esther' based on the years of Xerxes' reign.

In fact, Amestris was probably Vashti. The Persian name Vashti includes two consonants, 'v' and 'sh', not found in Greek, which could quite conceivably have been corrupted to 'm' and 's' in transcription.

What do we know about Amestris/Vashti from Herodotus? She was exceptionally strong-willed and ruthless. When her son ascended the throne, she became a veritable dragon of a queen mother, demanding that he brutally punish anyone to whom she took exception. When she got older she is supposed to have buried 14 Persian boys alive as a gift to the gods of the underworld, hoping that the Dark Powers would accept their lives in return for hers.

As we have said, when we are first introduced to Xerxes – or rather, to Ahasuerus[1] – by the author of 'Esther', it is in connection with a great banquet he is throwing for his

---

1. From here on I shall refer to the king by his Hebrew name (Ahasuerus) except when quoting from passages by Greek authors.

subjects (Esther 1:3). Banquets have always been a popular way for oriental kings to demonstrate their wealth, and indeed feasting is an important motif in the book of Esther – another factor contributing to its carnival atmosphere. In 1971 the Shah of Persia, who regarded himself as successor to the Achaemenid emperors, held celebrations to mark the 2,500th anniversary of the founding of the Persian empire by Cyrus the Great. In a lavish city of tents near the ruins of Persepolis, he entertained nearly half the world's monarchs and heads of state. They were all accommodated in luxurious tents around a magnificent fountain, and the apartments of the shah himself and his empress were lined with purple velvet curtains and purple carpets.

In some translations it sounds as though Ahasuerus' banquet lasted six months! But it was probably the exhibitions of the king's treasures which lasted this long, and the banquet was their culmination.

A banquet of this kind could last several days, however. In the West we aren't used to this. If a party lasts beyond the small hours and goes on into the next day, we reckon it must have been a resounding success. But in many parts of the developing world it's still quite common for wedding celebrations to go on for days. Families actually bankrupt themselves, and we might be tempted to ask how people living in such communities ever have time to do anything other than go to weddings!

In fact on this occasion there were *two* banquets, one for the nobles and officials of his empire (Esther 1:3) and then one for all the people who lived in the citadel of Shushan, 'from the least to the greatest' (1:5). This has to mean that one of the people invited was Esther's cousin Mordecai himself, and, presumably, Esther along with him. She must have been something like twelve years old at the time – exactly the sort of age at which girls are inclined to develop crushes on handsome and powerful men. So it's likely that Ahasuerus wasn't the only one looking forward with relish to the royal banquet. . . .

*   *   *

Esther had been caught up in a whirlwind of excitement ever since the day the official invitation arrived. What a fantastic treat it would be, to step inside the palace of Ahasuerus himself, to tread upon the mosaic pavements of porphyry, marble and mother-of-pearl, where previously only the members of the imperial household had trodden! To drink from a golden goblet while reclining on a golden couch beneath the billowing awnings that festooned every pillar; to be waited upon by slaves who on every other day of their lives served persons of royal blood. What a contrast everything would make with her cousin's home, which was as plain and unassuming as it was possible for anywhere to be, to the point of austerity. As a devout Jew living in exile among decadent Gentiles, Mordecai was determined that every area of his life should make a statement to the effect that he and his adoptive daughter were different from their pagan neighbours. Nor would he have any decoration in his house that might be interpreted as idolatrous.

Esther understood this perfectly well, and yet there was a part of her that longed to be just like everybody else. Or rather, not like *everybody* else, but like the wealthy ones. Sometimes she would study her reflection in a pool, or in one of those bronze mirrors which were sold in the market but which Mordecai would never allow her to buy. Then she would sigh when she saw herself wearing her plain home-spun robe, and she would dream of bringing home a bale of

fine linen from which she might make the kind of gown that
Persian ladies wore. She would wonder what her eyes would
look like painted with kohl or malachite, and in the privacy
of her room she would pile up her thick black hair on top of
her head then tease out wispy tendrils to curl saucily about
her face. Esther was pretty and she knew it, and in her more
generous moments she knew that Mordecai only wanted
what was best for her. But there were other times – usually
when she was missing her parents badly – that she was
starting to regard him as something of a spoilsport.

And so she'd been counting off the days until the
morning of the royal banquet arrived. She was so excited
that she could scarcely fasten her cloakpins, and pricked her
fingers more than enough times on their sharp points. For
once she had been permitted to wear her best dress and
some of the jewellery her mother had left her, and she was
sure that this was going to be the most wonderful day of her
life. Meanwhile in the palace Ahasuerus was thinking the
same thing, but he couldn't have been more wrong.

Esther would not have been able to attend the banquet at
all if her cousin had not had a kinswoman prepared to take
her, for Ahasuerus was to entertain the men while his wife
Vashti played hostess to the ladies. Fortunately Mordecai
did have such a kinswoman, and there was nothing to
prevent Esther from attaining her heart's desire.

Nor did her initial impressions of the royal palace
disappoint her. She was awestruck by everything she saw,
and amused to think that her cousin would be disgusted by
the ostentation. Ahasuerus' palace was surrounded by towering walls, every inch of which was covered with panels of
glazed bricks in green, blue, deep red and gold. Running
along these walls were beautiful friezes, some depicting
heroes stalking lions, or ranks of liveried soldiers, or
endless processions of the king's foreign subjects come to

bring him tribute. Others showed birds and fish and fantastic animals: gryphons, creatures with goat's horns, lion's forepaws and tail, and eagle's claws where the hindpaws ought to have been. There were soaring columns crowned with exquisitely carved stags or bulls, which boasted long curving horns and appeared so graceful and lifelike you could imagine that at any moment they might spring up and bound away, leaving the ornately plastered ceiling to come crashing down upon the floor below. Wherever you looked, you would see the emblem of Ahura-Mazda himself, a disc representing the sun, with out-stretched wings on either side. Sometimes the disc had a human figure inside it; this symbolized the Achaemenid king in union with his god.

Also, there were the sumptuous decorations put up specially for the banquet, in the gardens as well as inside the buildings. Among the fountains and the fruit trees and the formal beds of flowers there were blue and white linen awnings fastened with silver rings to marble pillars. There were couches of gold and silver arranged on mosaic pavements made out of precious stones: turquoise, feldspar and mother-of-pearl.

Even more fascinating than the palace itself were its people. How Esther stared at the perfumed harem ladies with their fabulous clothing and jewels; and the eunuchs, some old and bald and run to fat, others so young and slender and handsome you couldn't be sure if they were eunuchs at all, or unusually beautiful boys. And some of them were looking at *her*. . . .

Then there was the food! Esther was happily putting all sorts of exotic-looking delicacies onto her plate, while her kinswoman took them off again just as quickly because they weren't kosher. Wine was flowing freely too: the rule for drinking was 'no restrictions', which meant that everyone could drink as much – or as little – as they wished; there was no compulsion, as there often was, to drink the same amount as the host. How dreadfully dull and strict Mordecai's house seemed in comparison; what a pious old fuddy-duddy he seemed to be.

However, Esther was about to find out that the sweetness of over-indulgence can all too quickly turn sour.

3

A Banquet and a Banishing

Esther was starting to fall asleep. She had eaten so much that she never wanted to see another plate of sweetmeats or another sherbet dessert in all her life. She had even been allowed some wine, which had gone straight to her head and made her sleepier than ever. With her chin resting on her arms on the table in front of her, and her eyelids drooping, she let the grown-ups' conversation wash pleasantly over her; the women's shrill voices and raucous laughter seemed to be coming from somewhere very far away.

All of a sudden, things went horribly quiet. Puzzled, Esther raised her heavy head and saw that everyone else had turned to stare at the top table, where Queen Vashti was sitting with her ladies-in-waiting and her closest friends. Seven of the king's eunuchs had entered the hall and their spokesman appeared to be engaged in a heated dispute with Vashti herself! As they argued, Vashti's expression grew haughtier, and her cheeks more flushed with anger. Eventually she turned her face away from the eunuchs altogether and covered it with her veil. The eunuchs left; the tension subsided; gradually conversation resumed and everyone pretended that the incident had never taken place. Everyone, that is, except Esther, who tugged at her kins-woman's sleeve and pestered her to explain what was going on. But nobody seemed to know.

*   *   *

What was in fact going on was a battle of wills between the most powerful man on the planet and his queen. Battles of the will emerge as just as important a feature of the book of Esther as banquets! The commotion had come about because Ahasuerus had apparently ordered his wife to abandon her female guests, and, wearing her royal crown, to parade her beauty for the appreciation of the men.

But why on earth would Ahasuerus make such a bizarre request? It would be enough to offend a Western woman, let alone one of her sisters in the Middle East where a woman's beauty is still strictly reserved for her husband.

The custom of keeping women in seclusion has found its most extreme expression in the wearing of the all-enveloping Islamic 'chador'. The word is Persian in origin, and of course Persia (present-day Iran) is one of the parts of the world where this costume is most commonly seen. But the origins of the custom are certainly pre-Islamic. It's interesting to note that many Islamic women find wearing a chador liberating rather than restricting: they claim that it prevents men from seeing them as sex-objects and compels them to respect women as human beings instead. I think that if they had put their case to Vashti just at the moment when Ahasuerus' eunuchs turned up, she might well have conceded their point.

It's also interesting that throughout its history Persia/Iran seems to have experienced periods of quite remarkable tolerance and 'Westernization' alternating with periods of extreme religious fundamentalism. We witnessed the latter under Khomeini, the former under the Shah. Now it seems that the pendulum is beginning to swing in favour of tolerance again – the Iranian Government has recently distanced itself from the *fatwa* against Salman Rushdie. Under the early Achaemenid kings, tolerance had been the norm; Ahasuerus' demand for Vashti to appear before his guests was to set in motion a chain of events that was to lead Persia rapidly in the opposite direction.

The most obvious explanation for Ahasuerus' imprudent behaviour in this episode is the fact that he was drunk – Esther 1:10 tells us that he was 'in high spirits from wine'. As a result he may simply have been acting in unthinking response to the taunts of his drinking-companions. We can readily imagine them clamouring, 'Your Majesty, for six months you've been showing off your treasures, yet you've kept the most beautiful of all your possessions firmly under lock and key! How about exhibiting *her*?' Perhaps they *dared* the king to bring his wife before them.

This incident thus provides a good example of why as Christians we are exhorted by the Apostle Paul: 'Do not get drunk with wine, which leads to debauchery, but instead be filled with the Spirit' (Ephesians 5:18). In other words, it isn't so much drunkenness in itself that Paul is condemning, but what it leads to. Alcohol suppresses our inhibitions – and some of them are very *useful* inhibitions. Self-control is a fruit of the Spirit, but wild abandonment comes from the fruit of the vine and can all too easily undo the work of God within us.

You may well be wondering: 'But what counts as drunkenness? How much alcohol should I allow myself to have?' Quite apart from the fact that the answer to this question will be different for everyone, it's really the wrong question to be asking. So many Christians waste so much time hovering over this kind of dividing line. Each of them is like a child walking along by the edge of the sea with his shoes on, one foot on the beach and one in the water, wondering how far he dare go before his socks get wet and his mother tells him off. They want to have one foot in the sea of spiritual experience while the other is planted on the shifting sand of worldliness.

The truth is that we only really find out what Christianity is all about and begin to have an impact on those around us when we stop teetering on the brink and plunge into the ocean of God's love with everything we've got. Where is the sense in our wasting our time worrying about what God will let us get away with, as though he were some kind of Victorian schoolmaster, when all the time he is our loving Father who has a plan for each of our lives that represents the absolute best that could ever happen to us? Jesus came to offer us life in abundance (John 10:10), not a set of rules and regulations to nit-pick over as the Pharisees did. We are called to commit ourselves to God lock, stock and barrel, and trust him for everything; once we have come to know him well enough, through the nurturing of a vibrant relationship with him, we won't be in any doubt as to what counts as life in abundance and what constitutes dangerous excess. The satisfaction and sense of fulfilment that derive from knowing absolutely that we are doing God's will are so complete that we should see no further need to drug ourselves against life's frustrations.

Yes, it's true that Jesus enjoyed a drink as much as the next man, and was happy to see others enjoying God's provision in this way too, otherwise he would never have turned water into wine – and jolly good wine at that (John 2:1–11)! But abundance and abuse are two entirely different things, and what God has in store for us is a million times more exciting than alcohol.

Yet again, though, there may be more to Ahasuerus'

demand than simple intoxication. Before Persia had come into close contact with Babylon it seems that Persian men and women had mixed freely. King and queen would have dined together, with their guests of both sexes. (In a more intimate setting, this sort of arrangement probably still persisted, as we'll see later on.) It was among the Semitic peoples, Babylonians included, that segregation of men and women was customary; and if there was anything that made Ahasuerus' blood boil, it was seeing Semitic customs prevail over Aryan. He felt the same about Semitic influence as Ayatollah Khomeini used to feel about American! So perhaps when he rose to his companions' bait it was because in his inebriate state he was saying to himself: 'In the good old days Vashti would have been sitting here by my side, so why on earth *shouldn't* you all have the pleasure of seeing her? What's the use of my having a beautiful bride if no one envies me for it?'

Vashti, however, had refused his request. She had publicly snubbed his seven eunuchs, in the full hearing of her attendants and bosom companions. How horrified the latter must have been by her behaviour – and yet how thrilled at the same time. For a woman flagrantly to disobey her husband, and to do it in front of guests, was unheard of – and when her husband was the *king*. . . .! It was as though the very pillars upon which ancient Middle Eastern society was built had been set tottering like a flimsy cottage in an earthquake.

So why had Vashti defied her husband in this way? I think most women today would find the answer to this question too blindingly obvious to bother putting it into words. They might well conclude that Vashti deserves the title of 'feminist champion' more than Esther, in refusing to disport herself in front of these lascivious lager louts.

But astonishingly, some early commentators (all men)

found her refusal so baffling that they postulated that she must have been ugly, or even a leper! This, in spite of the fact that the text expressly tells us that Vashti was lovely to look upon (Esther 1:11). Others have suggested that the same verse implies that Vashti was ordered to appear wearing *only* her crown! One rabbinic commentator suggested that the Persian queen must have lived a wild life in her younger days; that once upon a time she had been in the habit of dancing naked in front of men, so she had brought all this upon herself.

By the same token Vashti has been severely criticized in some quarters for not submitting to Ahasuerus' wishes regardless of how offensive she found them, since he was her husband, and king to boot. But we shouldn't be too hasty in condemning her in this way. The author of 'Esther' neither praises nor criticizes her action.

The Jewish writer Rachel Brownstein observes[1] that we often tend to look at biblical women in pairs (Sarah and Hagar, Rachel and Leah, etc.), making comparisons between the two in favour of the former against the latter, the chosen against the unchosen. The same is often done with Esther and Vashti. But in exalting one of each pair and slighting the other, we don't do justice to the text, in any one of these cases. Sarah isn't the 'goodie' and Hagar the 'baddie' at all; neither is Leah or Vashti to be despised. It's true that in Jewish Purim pageants all the little girls want to play Esther, and the role of Vashti is very much a consolation prize, if that. (The boys, on the other hand, vie for *all* the major male roles.) But perhaps we should all question our assumptions in the way we interpret Scripture. We should read what is there instead of what we think ought to be there.

Conversely, in this age of equality between the sexes, the

---

1. Christina Büchmann and Celina Spiegel (eds), *Out of the Garden* (Ballentine Books, 1994).

idea of the Christian wife 'submitting to her husband' in *any* circumstances has caused offence to many. In the Church of England Marriage Service women now have a choice as to whether they promise to obey their husbands or not. Since Keith and I married in an independent church, we didn't have a very clear idea as to what the service consisted of, and it hadn't occurred to us to find out in advance exactly what the minister was going to ask us to promise! I didn't know whether I was going to have to obey Keith for the rest of my days until the moment came for me to say 'I do'.

But I didn't much mind whether I promised to obey him or not, because I knew that the question of obedience ought never to arise. Yes, there is a sense in which the husband is head of the household. In Ephesians 5:23 Paul reminds us that a husband has authority over his wife just as Christ has authority over the church. And if an important decision has to be made over which husband and wife simply cannot agree, someone has to have the final say, otherwise destructive strife will inevitably result. But if a husband has to *compel* his wife to toe the line, I reckon their marriage is already in deep trouble. Adam and Eve were meant to be partners, not master and slave. And as Paul goes on to point out (Ephesians 5:25), the husband is meant to love his wife as Christ loved the church, laying down his very life for her. The ultimate ideal is that we all submit to each other, out of our reverence for Christ (Ephesians 5:21).

A rather wacky possibility is that Vashti refused Ahasuerus' request as a *joke*, because she thought he'd been joking too! There were many festivals in the ancient world and in the Middle Ages, such as the Roman Saturnalia or medieval Feast of Fools, where for the duration of the festivities social hierarchies were turned upside down: masters were ordered around by their servants, employers by their employees, etc. It was a sort of safety valve in strictly feudal societies, such as Persia was, and prevented revolution.

Whether Vashti's refusal was justifiable or not, it was potentially very dangerous. Achaemenid Persia, in common with just about every other society in antiquity, had a culture very much based upon the concept of honour. This means that it was vital to the preservation of one's status and to one's own sense of self-worth that one never accepted any kind of insult from anyone, however trivial, without ensuring that an equal or greater snub was delivered in return. There is a brilliant example of this in the ancient Greek epic the *Iliad*, where the hero Achilles flatly refuses to fight for his country because his commanding officer has insulted his honour by appropriating the slave girl whom Achilles has been awarded as booty. Achilles demands the girl's return and his commander's abject apology; when he doesn't get his way, his stubbornness leads directly to the tragic death of his own best friend.

Of course, many modern societies operate a code of honour. Anyone who has spent any length of time in the Middle East or in parts of Asia will know this to be true. But it is equally true of gangland culture in America, and even in some parts of Britain where there has been little movement of population over the centuries and the local culture is still in many ways tribal. Family feuds can continue for generations because no one is prepared to forgive and forget until scores are seen to be settled.

I am in no doubt that it is largely due to 2,000 years of Christian influence that much of Western society has to some extent moved beyond this way of thinking. It was Jesus who told us to love our enemies, to turn the other cheek, to go the extra mile – all actions which would previously have been regarded by most people as signs of weakness, and represent the very antithesis of honour culture. And as we have already seen, Paul encouraged us to submit to one another out of our reverence for Christ. Though the West has squandered much of its Christian heritage, it still values the virtues of mercy and forbearance and recognizes that peace is better than war. Although many non-Christians would quite rightly argue that you don't need to be a Christian to admire or exhibit such virtues, it is Christianity that taught mankind to value them in the first place.

Certainly in Ahasuerus' and Vashti's Persia it was honour that was valued above all else. Ahasuerus would have been appallingly shamed by his wife's refusal of his request. To accept it would have meant losing face in front of his guests, and this could not be tolerated, as it would bring disgrace not only upon him but upon the Achaemenid dynasty. And if there was one thing that caused Ahasuerus to lose sleep at night, it was the fear of being proven unworthy of the kings who had gone before him.

Vashti must surely have known what a perilous step she had taken in insulting her husband's honour – unless she genuinely thought (as suggested above) that he ought to be able to take a joke. The fact that he *couldn't* may be due to the fact that this was the last day of the festivities (Esther 1:10), and on the last day of any Saturnalia-type festival there was always the danger that society would not return to normal afterwards; that the downtrodden, having acquired a taste of freedom, would not be content to return whence they had come.

Whatever lay behind it, Vashti's insistence on this point of principle had disastrous consequences, just as Mordecai's equivalent intransigence was to cause potential disaster later in the book. This is another of its themes, in fact: principle versus pragmatism. Again, the book doesn't actually come down in favour of one or the other. All it does is show us that inflexibility does have serious consequences

– sometimes for others as well as ourselves. We ought to
think twice before leaping to the conclusion that it is
always, automatically right for us to 'stand up for our
principles'. Obviously there are circumstances in which we
have to: we would be compromising our very faith in God
if we did not. No one could say that in Shakespeare's
Measure for Measure Isabella ought to have slept with the
evil Angelo in order that he might set her brother free. But
in *King Lear* I've never quite understood why Lear's
youngest daughter doesn't wax lyrical about her love for
him, if that's what he wants to hear.

Vashti doesn't have to wait long to discover what the
consequences of *her* fierce adherence to principle are going
to be. . . .

*   *   *

Ahasuerus had never been so angry in all his life. When his
eunuchs returned from the hall where the women were
feasting and told him that his wife had refused to do his
bidding, he could quite easily have strangled all seven of
them with his bare hands.

'How dare she!' he roared. 'How dare she!' Leaping from
his couch, he swept goblets, bowls and plates onto the floor,
and it was all that his companions could do to keep him
from overturning the very table at which they sat. Not yet
knowing the cause of his fury, most of his guests simply
gaped in astonishment, while Memucan, chief of the royal
advisors, sought to calm the enraged monarch by saying
softly in his ear, 'Your Majesty, let the members of your
Council retire with you to a private chamber, and there you
shall decide what must be done.'

At length, still spitting blood, the king agreed. He strode from the hall with his cape flying behind him and his seven noble counsellors in his wake.

'Well?' he demanded of them, once they had retired to his private apartments and closed the door. 'What does the law demand that I do with her?' For it was the custom that the king consult with his legal experts in all matters pertaining to law and justice.

For an interval none of them spoke. They shifted in their seats and read each other's eyes, mulling over in silence what might be deemed an acceptable response. The law in fact had nothing whatever to say upon the matter, for such a thing had never happened in all the history of Persia, nor had its likelihood ever been imagined.

Finally Memucan cleared his throat and announced, 'Your Majesty, Queen Vashti has wronged not only you but every one of your subjects, by making an attack upon the very fabric of your empire. For her conduct will become known to women everywhere, with the result that they will all despise their husbands and reject their rightful authority. The wives of commoners and noblemen alike will become rebellious, and there will be no end of disrespect and disharmony.'

At this point he paused to see how the king was reacting. Ahasuerus continued to fume, his painted eyes like smouldering coals beneath his brows. So Memucan concluded, 'Therefore my lord, if it please you, issue a royal decree, and let it be written in the laws of the Medes and Persians which cannot be repealed, that Vashti is never again to enter your presence. When the edict is published throughout your realm, women will respect their husbands as they always have done and always should, from the least to the greatest.'

*   *   *

Memucan's advice pleased Ahasuerus. It pleased him very much. Without further ado, Queen Vashti was deposed (Esther 1:12–22). We aren't told whether she was literally put out into the street, or merely relegated to the rank of concubine and kept within the harem. (Personally I think the latter more likely.) Even if she *was* put out in the street, her children would have remained at the palace and not necessarily been disinherited. Children in Persia were seen as belonging entirely to their fathers.

We have just seen that her demise comes about as a result of the counsel given to Ahasuerus by his seven advisors (not the same people as his seven eunuchs), who see in Vashti's refusal of her husband's request a dangerous precedent which could lead to marital chaos all over the empire, with women everywhere telling their husbands where to put their orders. Their reaction is almost comical, but then so was Ahasuerus' pathetic situation. The most powerful man on the planet plainly couldn't keep control within his own household; this did not augur well for the future of his empire.

One of the reasons why the author Rachel Brownstein likes Vashti's story so much is the fact that it demonstrates the paranoia of tyrants everywhere, and indicates that one woman's rebellion is inclined to make all men feel threatened. Vashti's career bears witness to the cruel constraints which have all too commonly limited women's chances of success in the world; we so often feel obliged to please, rather than to be ourselves.

So, who was actually running the show: Ahasuerus or his Council? If he *was* over-dependent on the latter – and it seems that he was – why was this the case? Two possibilities present themselves: (1) it was simply because of his insecurity and weakness of personality; (2) he was as much a 'victim of the system' as anyone else. Though theoretically the most powerful man on the planet, in practice he was as restricted in what he could do as the lowliest of his subjects. He wasn't only hemmed in by laws, but by astrological considerations. His advisors were men who 'understood the times' (Esther 1:13); in other words they were well versed in astrology and fate, and the king would be expected to act in accordance with their directions and predictions.

Probably at least some of them were magi. The magi constituted a mysterious and rather sinister order, whose origins were probably pre-Zoroastrian, and it was very much feared. It's no coincidence that the word 'magic' originates with the magi, who certainly practised it.

Although few Christians today are familiar with the culture of ancient Persia, we have all come across the magi because of their appearance in Matthew's Gospel in connection with the birth of Christ. I should like to take a few moments to examine their role in the Nativity story, not only because it is fascinating in itself, but because it has an important bearing on the concepts of fate and destiny, which we shall be discussing more fully in due course.

I used to find the magi's involvement in Jesus' birth narrative very perplexing, because when I became a Christian as a teenager I was told it was wrong to read my horoscope. I thought, 'But the magi practised astrology.' (Yes, *astrology*, not astronomy, and it led them to Jesus!) I couldn't find any light to shed on my perplexity until I read *The Magi* by Adrian Gilbert,[1] and it dawned on me that the visit of the magi may not have been a good thing! It led to the massacre of the Innocents, and to Jesus' parents having to flee with him to Egypt. Tradition (not the Bible) tells us that the magi's gifts represent Jesus' royalty, divinity and passion, but Adrian Gilbert suggests another interpretation

---

1. Adrian Gilbert, *The Magi* (Bloomsbury Publishing, 1996).

altogether. He connects the gifts closely with the temptations faced by Jesus in the wilderness and says that they represent the gifts of the planets associated astrologically with Jesus' birth: magic, preservation of life, and worldly power and wealth. These are precisely the areas in which Jesus was tempted by Satan, but in overcoming these temptations Jesus rose above his astrological fate to find his true destiny. Also, when he submitted to crucifixion he symbolically threw these gifts back whence they had come; he specifically refused to use magic to jump down from the cross, he willingly gave up his life, and though crucified as 'King of the Jews' he had refused all political power and continued to do so right until the end. Of course, the gospel narrative does not lay any blame at the feet of the magi, who were clearly guided by God to avoid the murderous Herod (Matthew 2:12), and we are left to draw our own conclusions.

The contrast between fate and destiny, and the rivalry between astrology and faith in God, constitute another important theme of 'Esther'. To Gilbert, fate and destiny have crucially different meanings. Fate is passive, destiny active. Our fate represents what is likely to become of us as a result of things outside our control: our genes, back-ground, upbringing – perhaps even our horoscope. But the challenge to each of us is to do as Jesus did: to break out of the grip of fate, to find our destiny, which represents what each of us is meant to become, in God. Gilbert does not claim to be a Christian, but what he says makes more sense from a Christian viewpoint than from any other. It also explains why horoscopes are to be avoided: if we get hung up on trying to learn about our fate, we'll never enter into what *God* wants for us. This is one of the most important messages contained in the letters of Paul. We don't need secret knowledge; we need faith.

Going back to Ahasuerus, the suggestions given above as

to why he was over-dependent on his advisors may both be true. A strong king like Darius would never have let astrological considerations get in his way. Those characters in 'Esther' who rely on astrology and the casting of lots emerge as the bad guys, and whenever Ahasuerus follows their advice he gets himself into serious trouble and does things which he later deeply regrets. Ahasuerus is not the villain of the piece, but he *is* led badly astray. Haman (whom we have yet to meet, but who most certainly *is* the villain) and Mordecai, his enemy, hold radically opposing worldviews: to Haman, fate is everything; to Mordecai everything is part of a pattern of which God is in ultimate control (see Esther 4:14). God had a special purpose for the Jews, and this was not to be thwarted by any man.

When we as readers see Ahasuerus being led astray in this fashion very early on in the book, it prepares us to accept the plausibility of what happens later.

Vashti's banishment is 'written into the laws of the Medes and Persians' – which means that it is made irrevocable. (There is another instance of exactly the same sort of thing in Daniel 6:12.) We need to remember this little snippet of information about the nature of Persian law – it too will become highly significant in due course.

We are already beginning to appreciate how 'tight' the plot of 'Esther' actually is. Every piece of information is made to work as hard as it possibly can: a single incident carries a great deal of weight, developing theme, character and plot all at once like the very best political thriller. We as readers have to work hard too if we are to get the most out of the book; we can't afford to forget any of the details which the author imparts to us along the way.

4

The Beauty Contest with a Difference

Ahasuerus, Great King of Persia, master of half the known
world, lay in bed alone. His bed was the largest and the
most ornate piece of furniture which anyone could ever
dream of possessing, but the lonely young king, sleepless
and restless in the night, was wishing it were smaller, and
not so cold. For the place beside him where his lovely wife
Vashti should have lain was empty, and it was as much his
own fault as that of his confounded counsellors. Anger and
insecurity had caused him to follow Memucan's ill-
considered advice and banish her from his sight. And
because he was King of Persia, and his word was law –
irrevocable law – she was never coming back.

Of course, he could have sent for any one of his countless
concubines, who would willingly have attempted to warm
his bed and inflame his desire. But he knew that it would do
no good. Vashti – beautiful, proud, spirited Vashti – was the
woman he loved, yet in a single misguided moment he had
thrown his happiness away.

More than three years had passed since the fateful
banquet – an occasion to which he had looked forward with
unqualified relish, but which had ended in unmitigated
disaster. Three years of loneliness and failure, during which
everything he had tried to do had gone wrong; three years,

in which not one of the nights he had spent with other women had brought him anything more than fleeting carnal pleasure.

It wasn't that he had not tried to put the past behind him. He really had done his best to pick up the pieces and get on with the rest of his life. Urged on by the most ambitious of his cousins he had planned and undertaken a major invasion of Greece, hoping to succeed where his father had failed in bringing that stubborn little nation of bickering city states under Persian control. But his army and navy had been destroyed. Even now he couldn't believe that it had happened, nor understand how – when the Greeks had been so hopelessly outnumbered and had lacked any form of centralized authority – they could have repelled the hosts of the Great King! But happen it had, plunging Ahasuerus himself into the depths of a depression from which he had not yet begun to recover. Tossing and turning upon his bed, he doubted that he ever would.

There were those who had sought to bring him comfort, and for that he had been grateful. Yet somehow he had been unable to show his gratitude without everything going sour. On his way back from Greece he had stopped off at the city of Sardis, spending some time there with the family of his younger brother. His brother's wife had been kind to him, visiting his chambers herself to bring him food when he could not face eating anywhere else. She had listened with endless patience to his catalogue of woes, so that he had poured out his heart to her without restraint.

Surely he wasn't to blame, therefore, for having concluded that the woman was in love with him? Surely it had been *her* fault for sending out all the wrong signals? He had only offered her what he sincerely believed she'd been asking for: how could he have known that she would put up such a resistance? The whole business was so sordid, but not as sordid as it had become when he had been introduced to her adolescent daughter. So like her mother, the girl had been. So gentle, so pretty, and yet so young, with her breasts only starting to show, and the bloom of youth so bright upon her cheeks. How could any man have resisted such doe-eyed innocence when it was so willingly offered?

The one thing it seemed the girl did not have in common with her mother was her mother's firm resolve to repel Ahasuerus' advances. It was just as well that he'd been rushed back to Shushan by his scandalized advisors, who by now were fervently wishing that they had never recommended the deposing of Vashti in the first place. . . .

*   *   *

It is Herodotus who tells us about the Persian expedition against Greece, about the king's depression over its failure, and about his scandalous behaviour while staying with his brother's family in Sardis. But as we shall soon see, his account meshes very well with that of the biblical author.

I think we can be fairly certain from the text of 'Esther' that Ahasuerus had loved Vashti very much. When his rage had subsided after the banquet, 'he remembered Vashti' we are told in Esther 2:1, and in that simple, achingly poignant little sentence, all the king's misery is summed up. For he who embodied the law now found himself at its mercy.

It fell eventually to the king's advisors, who were largely to blame for landing their royal master in his sorry predicament, to suggest a way out of it. And what they came up with was basically a beauty contest involving every eligible maiden in the realm (Esther 2:2–4). A thorough search would be undertaken, a bevy of beautiful maidens would be brought to the palace, and the girl who pleased the king the most would be crowned as the new Queen of Persia.

One idea behind this contest may have been that the king could never truly be content if he suspected that someone, somewhere in his enormous empire, had a wife more gorgeous than he had. But uppermost in the advisors' minds, I should imagine, was a determination to find the girl who most resembled Vashti. Maybe Ahasuerus had said, 'I'll never find anyone else like her . . .' and his advisors had responded, 'Why not? Why don't you let us try?'

We can't tell from the text exactly when this happened. It just says 'later'. We might be forgiven for concluding that the contest got under way as soon as Vashti had been sent packing, or at least as soon as Ahasuerus had slept off his hangover.

In fact probably quite a while elapsed between the banquet and the beginning of the search for Vashti's replacement. The banquet had taken place in the third year of Ahasuerus' reign (Esther 1:3), but it was not until the seventh year that Esther was brought before him (Esther 2:16). I suppose it could be that the contest itself lasted up to four years and that Ahasuerus slept with a different girl every night during all that time – but his harem would have been well and truly overcrowded by then!

It seems to me to be much more likely that those intervening years were taken up with Persia's second major invasion of Greece. We know from other sources that Xerxes/Ahasuerus was crowned king in 486 BC, and that his Greek expedition was in preparation between 483 and 480, when the invasion actually took place. It was also during these three years that Babylon revolted from Persian rule; Xerxes crushed the revolt with horrific savagery, and from this time onward no longer styled himself King of Persia,

Babylon and Egypt (thus recognizing these two peoples as belonging to a category superior to that of other subject nations), but King of Persia only. (Egypt had revolted and been subdued at the very beginning of his reign.)

It's interesting that in the Greek playwright Aeschylus' tragedy *The Persians*, when what is left of the expedition limps home after its defeat at the hands of the Greek states, Xerxes seems to have no wife to comfort him. We hear plenty about the wives of his men, but Xerxes himself has only his mother Atossa (Hutaosa) to turn to, despite the fact that we know from Herodotus that Xerxes had already been married to Amestris/Vashti for some time.

As we mentioned earlier in this chapter, we also know from Herodotus that Xerxes was exceedingly depressed after this defeat – another attempt to rival his predecessors had failed. During the expedition itself he had shown signs of mental instability; when a bridge he'd had built across the Hellespont (the Dardanelles) was wrecked in a storm, he had ordered that the sea should receive 300 lashes and have fetters thrown into it, and he'd even sent men to brand it with hot irons. His cruel streak showed itself on the same occasion: he ordered that the men responsible for building the bridge should have their heads chopped off.

Xerxes' father Darius had failed in *his* attempt to take Greece ten years previously (it was during Darius' expedition that the famous Battle of Marathon was fought), so Xerxes ought to have thought twice before attempting it. But in Herodotus, as in 'Esther', Xerxes/Ahasuerus is lured all too willingly into following imprudent advice – in this case that of his hot-headed cousin Mardonius, who wanted to be the governor of any newly acquired territories. According to Mardonius, Europe was such a beautiful place that it was 'too good for anyone except the Persian king'!

On his return home, Herodotus tells us, Xerxes lingered

at Sardis, which led to his having 'inappropriate relations' with his niece, after the girl's own mother had spurned his advances. Somehow President Clinton's alleged sexual misdemeanours pale into insignificance when compared with the sort of thing Herodotus describes. Mind you, they are pretty insignificant compared with what King David did, as well! (See 2 Samuel 11.) Perhaps it was the discovery of this sordid affair that gave rise to the decision that a new bride should be found for the lonely king as a matter of urgency, before his desperation drove him to do something even worse.

We don't know exactly how the contest was organized. All we are told (in Esther 2:3) is that Ahasuerus decided to 'appoint commissioners in every province of his realm' who were to arrange for any suitably lovely girls they identified to be brought to the palace at Shushan.

I wonder how our heroine felt when news of the commissioners' enquiries reached her ears? I like to think she was excited. She knew perfectly well that she was pretty – astonishingly so. She was a virgin, with an impeccable reputation. Mordecai's hawk-eyed supervision had made sure of that. And I have a strong suspicion that she was heartily sick of the strict regime he imposed upon her, making her cook and clean, and sew and spin, in preparation for life as a dutiful Jewish wife. She wanted jewels and perfumes, fine gowns and golden sandals; she wanted love, and passion, to lose her virginity in the arms of a man of substance and experience . . . and there was no one richer or more experienced than the king himself, who was young, lean, lithe and handsome to boot. In her naive and eager mind, it was high time to say goodbye for ever to Hadassah, the modest Jewish maiden, and hello to Esther, goddess of love and beauty. Provided that her name was brought to the commissioners' attention, she was confident that she could convince Ahasuerus to look no further.

Of course, she couldn't mention any of this to her friends, let alone to her strait-laced guardian. Her friends would have fallen about laughing, and Mordecai would have beaten her black and blue. Still, she could always dream. . . .

But how was any girl's name to come to the commissioners' notice? How were these illustrious men to identify suitable candidates for their scrutiny, in a society where fathers kept their daughters strictly in seclusion? Did the commissioners go from house to house demanding that all unmarried girls be brought out to them for inspection?

I'm reminded of a curious custom I came across while travelling in Turkey with a friend of mine one summer. Our guide pointed out some cola bottles cemented on to the roofs of the houses in a village we passed through, and told us that the shape of the bottle indicated the shape of the marriageable daughter of the household! A tall thin bottle denoted a tall thin girl, while a short fat bottle meant that a short fat girl lived within. When we asked what would happen if a father pretended that his daughter was tall and thin when really she was short and fat, our guide couldn't seem to grasp what we were saying. It took us some while to fathom the reason for his lack of comprehension. In rural Turkey it's considered *better* to be short and fat; no man would want a skinny, spindly bride in his bed, so why on earth would anyone want to pretend that this was the shape of his daughter?

Assuming that this custom did not already exist in Esther's day, I should imagine that the commissioners pursued various lines of enquiry, and that for a variety of motives people told them where suitable girls might be found. Perhaps there was an element of vindictiveness involved in some cases: neighbours who did not get on may have sought to stir up trouble for one another, especially perhaps for those who belonged to certain ethnic minorities among the populace.

And once found by Ahasuerus' commissioners, was a girl simply seized by force? Or were her parents only too keen to have her off their hands and save her dowry into the bargain, especially if it meant that she could compete for the chance to be Queen of Persia?

A girl's chances of winning the competition were probably about as good as our chances of winning a substantial prize in the National Lottery. But the consequences of losing were considerably worse, since much more than the cost of a ticket was at stake. For those girls who were deflowered by Ahasuerus but not chosen as queen, the future would be more like widowhood than the life of a lottery winner. There would be a one-night honeymoon, then a lifetime eked out cooped up in the bowels of the Shushan harem. If it was anything like the Topkapi palace in Istanbul – which it probably was – the concubines' rooms were almost as dark and cramped as the cages of battery hens. Contemplating the practicalities of all this is no doubt one of the factors that has led some scholars to say that the whole of the book of Esther is a fabrication. The beauty contest is just too far-fetched, they say; it never could have happened.

Perhaps this is the time for us to address a little more seriously the question of what *kind* of book 'Esther' is, i.e. to what genre it belongs. For not all of the stories in the Bible are necessarily history, Jesus' parables being the best example. No one knows or cares whether there really was a man going from Jerusalem to Jericho who was mugged and left for dead, then rescued by a Samaritan. It's the moral of the story that matters, not its historicity. So might 'Esther' just be an elaborate parable about persecution and the survival of the Jewish race? Are we wasting our breath discussing its historicity, just as we might be if we staked our faith on a literal seven-day creation when the text doesn't necessarily demand a literal interpretation? Is 'Esther' satire, as the Jewish writer Celina Spiegel has suggested?[1] Satire as a genre didn't fully emerge until Roman times, but 'Esther' could be 'satirical' in the sense of a piece of writing cleverly crafted to mock the established order and turn everything on its head. Or is it a proto-historical novel? The first actual extant novel is Chariton's *Callirhoe*, probably written in the first century BC. Some Jews, even some very Orthodox ones, think 'Esther' *is* a novel.

The answer to this question is hardly as crucial as deciding whether or not the Gospels were intended as history; clearly they were and their authors' determination to convince us of their literal credibility is written all over them. But there is no suggestion anywhere in 'Esther' that the account is anything other than historical. And anyone reading the Sardis episode in Herodotus, to which I referred above (Herodotus, 9), will be amazed at how like 'Esther' it all sounds. True, Herodotus too has been accused of riding roughshod over facts in order to create entertaining tales – his book, just like 'Esther', would have been intended for reading aloud to audiences who could never have owned books of their own – but it's surprising how many of his yarns, even some of the more bizarre ones, have turned out not to be so fanciful after all. As they say, fact can be stranger than fiction.

By some means, then, Esther did come to the commissioners' attention, though we aren't told how. Certain commentators have suggested that Mordecai put her name forward himself. But the text doesn't give me this

---

1. Christina Büchmann and Celina Spiegel (eds), *Out of the Garden* (Ballentine Books, 1994).

impression, and I cannot see why on earth he would have wanted to do this – unless she was much more badly behaved than Scripture suggests! He wouldn't have wanted his little girl deflowered by a man who had already deflowered hundreds of others.

Later on in the book, when we realize just how right the position is in which Esther has found herself, Mordecai's reaction in Esther 4:14 (in effect: 'Aha! So *this* is why you were chosen to be queen!') implies that at the time when she had been identified and duly taken away, he had been baffled, unable to comprehend what God could be playing at.

And surely we've all been there! When I was miserable at university I couldn't understand why God had led me to such a dreadful place, but if I hadn't hated the way my subject was being taught I would never have switched to studying theology, which is certainly what I was meant to be doing. Likewise, when Keith and I were involved in church leadership and found ourselves totally out of our depth, we couldn't understand why God had let us be appointed to such an unsuitable position in the first place. But if he hadn't, we would never have learned some of the crucial lessons he was teaching us – in particular, that we needed to get to know *him* a whole lot better.

In fact this is another important theme of the book of Esther: what exactly *is* God playing at in his world? Why do things often seem to turn out so badly for his people, even when they genuinely try to live for him? Why can living as a Christian seem like such a struggle sometimes? Why doesn't God make life a bit easier for us once we've decided to dedicate ourselves to him, so that others will want to do the same? Evangelism would be so much more effective, we suppose, if our daily lives were full of miracles!

But God is nothing like as interested in what *happens* to us as he is in what we *become*. It isn't our circumstances that count, but how we respond to them. Our characters are God's works of art! And character is not built without struggle. Sometimes he wants to increase our faith, and faith is trusting God even when we can't see what he is doing. Sometimes we have to learn patience. Mordecai too had to learn it and in due course he was to find out precisely why Esther had been whisked off to the palace.

Presumably Mordecai had wanted Esther to marry a nice Jewish boy and have lots of stalwart Jewish sons; perhaps arrangements for her betrothal were already under way. Mordecai would certainly have felt responsible to Esther's late father for finding her a worthy match, as any man in his position at the time would have done. In fact he probably felt the weight of this responsibility more than most, because of his own ancestry. We're told that he belonged to the tribe of Benjamin, though he's also described as a 'man of Judah', for Judahite (or Jew) was beginning to have the same meaning it has today, rather than referring to just one tribe. We also learn that his grandfather had been a certain Shimei, and Kish had been the name of his great-grandfather. This almost certainly means that he was connected by blood to Saul, the first king of Israel who had reigned 500 years before. Saul had been a Benjamite; his father had been called Kish, and one of his relatives, Shimei, had won notoriety by cursing King David in public (2 Samuel 16).

We cannot prove this Saulide connection conclusively – and possibly neither could Mordecai himself, since many family records had been lost when Jerusalem fell (see Ezra 2:59–62). But since Saul is my all-time favourite character from the Bible, I became really excited when I found that he and Esther were probably related. If only he hadn't forfeited his throne because of his disobedience to God, she might have been a princess in her own right! And the connection of Mordecai and Esther with Saul isn't merely interesting. It becomes highly significant later in the story of their lives.

But I very much doubt whether guardian and ward would have seen eye to eye regarding the desirable qualities in a husband. I can quite believe that Esther would have gone happily to Ahasuerus' bed, if the alternative was to marry some docile, dull-witted son of a synagogue worthy, or a middle-aged business associate of her cousin's.

While we might have been able to sympathize with such an attitude on Esther's part, could we have condoned it? Are there circumstances in which marrying someone who does not share our religious beliefs might be OK? Many Christian girls ask themselves this question, especially those who belong to churches where there seems to be a dearth of eligible young men. Personally I don't think anyone can legislate for anyone else in this matter, and it is very unwise to build your whole theology of marriage on 2 Corinthians 6:14 ('Don't be unequally yoked with unbelievers'). There are no hard and fast rules about this, any more than there are about most aspects of Christianity. In a sense there is no such thing as Christian ethics!

You may think that this is rather a dangerous statement to make, but the New Testament is categorically not about rules and regulations. The whole point of the new covenant in Christ's blood is that obedience to the law has been superseded by grace, which constrains us to live our lives in fellowship with, and under the guidance of, the Holy Spirit. Even in the Old Testament, the Ten Commandments say 'you shall not' (future tense), not 'do not' (imperative). In other words, if you love God and your neighbour, you will automatically fulfil the law.

But going back to the question of marriage to a non-believer, why on earth would you want to join yourself in union with someone who is utterly different from you at the very profoundest level of your being? You would have to have very clear and specific guidance to do so, and it's all too easy to kid yourself into imagining that God is saying exactly what you think he ought to say. If you do this, the person who will suffer the most in the long run is yourself. When God guides us, he does it for our own good as much as for his. We resist him at our peril.

On reflection, though, I'm sure that whoever *did* have a choice in all this, Esther herself would not have done. She was a woman, and a very young woman at that. Most likely she was only in her early teens, or the odds are that she would have been married already. Somehow or other she was picked out and sent to the palace whether she liked it or not. At this point in the story, Mordecai instructs her to keep her Jewishness a secret.

How might this have been possible? Surely the commissioners would know whose house she'd been taken from, and they would have been at pains to check out who her guardian was? Surely they kept records of each girl's origins? There's nothing new about bureaucracy. The Babylonians in particular were obsessed by it, and they had taught the Persians everything they knew. Did Mordecai *lie* about his ancestry and that of his ward, and somehow get away with it? Did he claim to be a Babylonian, as his name would have suggested? Maybe it was he who dreamed up the equally Babylonian name 'Esther' for his adoptive daughter, when the commissioners asked him what she was called? We can only guess.

But why did Mordecai tell her to keep her Jewishness a secret? There doesn't seem to have been any sort of threat to Jews up until this time. Perhaps Mordecai was simply paranoid ('Oh, no! My poor little girl, all on her own in a palace full of pagans!'). Or perhaps he was aware of the king's dogmatic Zoroastrian convictions and his belief in the supremacy of the Aryan race. Mordecai must have realized that if he himself had to give Esther up, she would be much better off as queen than as concubine – and there was no way that Ahasuerus would knowingly let a Semite share his throne, let alone bear him heirs of mixed blood. So far the king's ideology had had no discernible impact on the lives of his Jewish subjects, but it may be that Mordecai was shrewd enough to realize that, with the right catalyst, everything could go sky-high. Ahasuerus was so easily swayed by his advisors' plausible eloquence, all it would take would be for a Jew-hater to rise far enough through the ranks. . . .

5

In the House of Hegai

Esther perched anxiously on the edge of a chair and tried not to bite her neatly filed nails. Only a heavy curtain separated the bedroom in which she was sitting from the reception room where her cousin and guardian was deep in conversation with the royal commissioners. Or rather, *they* were deep in conversation with *him*. For he would have little more influence over Esther's fate now than she would herself.

They were talking in hushed voices, so she could not hear what they were saying. But she knew that she had pleased them. It wasn't so much what they had said while looking her over, but what they hadn't said, and the way they had exchanged charged glances with one another above her bowed head. She supposed that she ought to have felt demeaned, being inspected like a horse, or a slave for sale in the marketplace – and indeed she *would* have resented the commissioners' appraisal if she had read criticism or disappointment in their eyes. But there had been nothing but approval. They had noted the smoothness of her skin, the luxuriance and weight of her glossy hair. Wordlessly they had admired her perfect white teeth, her almond eyes, the exquisite symmetry of her features, the way she held herself, with grace and poise. And she had found herself blossoming silently under their scrutiny, like a rosebud opening in the sunlight. Mordecai had no time for physical beauty; he was always telling her that beauty of the soul was what really counted, for that could keep on growing your whole life long whereas beauty of the body would only fade as time went by. So there was something quietly thrilling about having the finer qualities of her face and figure fully recognized and appreciated for what they were.

But now, waiting nervously for the outcome of her examination to be announced, Esther was no longer sure what she wanted it to be. Being spirited off to the royal palace and introduced into the presence of the Great King had been her waking dream for weeks, even for months. Now, when it seemed that the dream might actually come true, she was having second thoughts. She would have to say goodbye not only to Mordecai, but to everything she had ever known, and exchange familiarity for something uncertain and frightening. The regular pattern she had always lived by would be gone. There would be no more sabbaths, no more festivals, no more lessons from holy scripture. The laws of God, which she had learned to obey from babyhood and which governed the behaviour and expectations of those around her, would no longer be respected. She would have to eat strange food – food she had been taught was unclean. She might even be made to worship Ahasuerus' peculiar foreign god. Religion had been no more a preoccupation for Esther than it had been for any of her blithe little playmates, but suddenly she felt as though the solid ground on which she stood was melting like wax beneath her.

All at once she realized that the voices in the next room had fallen silent. A moment later the curtain that screened her from the menfolk was brushed aside, and the verdict on her future brusquely delivered. A litter was to be sent forthwith to convey her to the royal palace, where she would embark upon twelve months' preparation for her first (and unless she were phenomenally lucky, her last) night with the Persian king.

Numb with the shock of it all, Esther found that she was able to do nothing but sit and wait for the litter to arrive. Somehow it seemed that in recent days her entire life had become devoted to waiting. She had waited to see if her name would be brought to the commissioners' attention, then waited for them to keep their appointment; waited while they completed their inspection; waited again until they reached their verdict on her suitability. Now she was waiting to be taken to the palace; there she would wait twelve whole months before being introduced to the king.

Whatever could they be going to do to her, she wondered, that would take so long and make her so very much more beautiful? Would they squeeze her waist into corsets, and bind up her feet until they were the shape of the pointed slippers she had seen the noble lords and ladies wearing at the banquet? Would they feed her on sickly sherbet until she was as round and fat as a Babylonian fertility goddess, or did Ahasuerus like his women slender? Certainly Vashti had not been fat, as far as Esther could recall.

Then suddenly there was no more time for recalling or wondering about anything. For Mordecai's kinswoman had arrived to help Esther pack her belongings, and everything had become a whirlwind of activity. Instructions and reprimands came thick and fast; clothes were scooped out of chests and crammed into bags, despite the fact that Esther was quite convinced that she would not be allowed to wear such dowdy homespun stuff ever again – as if she would want to! Presently Mordecai himself appeared amid the chaos, pacing back and forth like a cornered beast and barking out orders of his own which she must be sure to remember at all times: don't eat this, don't touch that, don't forget to say your prayers every day, and above all, don't tell anyone you're Jewish. Esther just blinked and nodded, taking in barely half of what he was saying to her.

Just as the final bag was being fastened up, the litter arrived from the palace. With dour liveried officials standing by, the little family's tearful goodbyes were inevitably brief and awkward. But Esther's tears dried the most quickly. Borne aloft through the streets where her erstwhile playmates still walked in the dust and the squalor, she lay back among the silken cushions and felt like a queen already.

Of course, Esther had been to the palace once before. But this time everything was different. Whisked away from the spacious halls with their soaring columns and spectacular friezes, she was taken behind the scenes into places no outsider ever saw.

Like everyone else in Shushan, Esther had heard a great deal about Ahasuerus' harem, but most of it had been romanticized nonsense or wild speculation. Facts had been harder to come by: for example, Esther had not previously been aware that there were actually *two* harems – one for girls such as herself who hadn't yet been to the king, and another for those who had, and who had thereby attained the status of royal concubine. Each of these harems was under the authority of one of Ahasuerus' two most trusted eunuchs, who went by the names of Hegai and Shaashgaz respectively. It was to Hegai that Esther was now presented, though if anyone had told her just then that he was destined to become her closest friend, she would not have believed it.

For Hegai was the most incredible creature Esther had ever laid eyes on. Somehow she'd assumed that all eunuchs were elderly, ugly, and running to fat. But Hegai was nothing of the kind. A dazzling vision of silk, brocade and jewels, with scarlet slippers on his feet and a carved dagger at his belt, his rampant hair and most of his face were swathed in the complex folds of his turban. In between, a pair of sultry kohl-rimmed eyes smouldered like cinders – all that remained of the fire of his stolen manhood. Outwardly proud and ravishingly beautiful, with his supercilious snarl and his acid tongue, he put fear in the heart of every girl in his charge. Yet inwardly ravaged and broken, he nursed a chronic grief for the parents he would never see again and for the children he would never have.

And so Hegai's were the perfectly manicured hands into which the apprehensive Esther was delivered, and under his expert tuition she embarked upon the year of preparation that would fit her for Ahasuerus' bed.

*   *   *

In common with Esther herself, we might be forgiven for asking why a whole year of elaborate treatments should be deemed necessary, when just about everyone our heroine had ever met had been bowled over by her beauty and charm already. But to the king and his commissioners, Esther belonged to the common herd, and must be purged of the pollution she had acquired by living in its midst. Besides, for the mightiest potentate in the world, the beauty imparted by nature could *never* be enough. The official line on feminine beauty at the Persian court was about as different from the view of Mordecai as it could possibly get, a view to be encapsulated in the words of the Apostle Peter: 'Your beauty should not come from outward adornment, such as braided hair, and the wearing of gold jewellery and fine clothes. Instead, it should be that of your inner self, the unfading beauty of a gentle and quiet spirit' (1 Peter 3:3).

Have you ever thought that this kind of inner beauty is in

fact every bit as visible on the outside as the superficial
beauty produced by artifice? Even with our modern chemi-
cals, we can't stop the wrinkles forming as we get older. But
we can affect *where* they form. Some very old people have
extraordinarily beautiful faces. The lines on our faces
reflect our personalities: the radiance of expression that is
acquired as a result of living in tune with God and experiencing the joy of daily fellowship with him cannot be faked
with make-up, and only grows more intense with every year
that passes. It's a bit like fate and destiny again. We can't do
much about the face we're born with, but we can do something about the one we will die with!

So much for Esther's appearance, and for the arrangements made to refine it. But what can we say about the
appearance of the palace that was to become her new home,
and how *this* was arranged? What was the purpose of each of
the many private rooms and apartments that no member
of the general public ever saw?

Today Susa is a confused jumble of ruins; it has proved
quite difficult for archaeologists even to restore the ground
plan. All the gold was looted by Alexander the Great, and of
the cedar panelling only dust remains. Fragments of the
glazed bricks can sometimes be fitted together like jigsaw
pieces, enabling us to catch a tiny glimpse of their former
splendour. But the glory of the Achaemenid emperors is
gone, along with that of every other dynasty that has placed
itself on such a lofty pedestal.

We do know that every Achaemenid king's palace had a
harem, or women's quarters. It is the book of Esther that
tells us Ahasuerus' harem at Shushan was divided into two
distinct parts (Esther 2:14), one for the girls who were still
virgins and one for the king's concubines. The concubines
might be sent for again whenever the king wished – or they
might not! But those whom the king found disappointing

couldn't simply be released into the community. They might already be pregnant by him, and besides, no honourable man in ancient Middle Eastern society would be prepared to put up with second-hand goods. So in a culture where the only way a respectable woman could find a meaningful role was within marriage, their lives were comprehensively ruined.

Esther 2:8 tells us that the virgins were in the charge of Hegai, and 2:14 that Shaashgaz was responsible for the concubines. It was Hegai's duty to check that each girl was fully prepared for her big night. The Talmud grudgingly admits that Ahasuerus, for all that he was 'wicked', 'did have something to his credit, namely that he did not perform his marital office by day'!

Hegai and Shaashgaz themselves were eunuchs; in other words, castrated males, who had been mutilated in this way for the express purpose of guarding the king's women. The Achaemenid kings were probably the first to castrate prisoners for this reason. The Greek writer Xenophon quotes Cyrus' argument that eunuchs made the most trustworthy servants, not only because they were incapable of getting the royal women into trouble, but because unlike 'real' men they weren't continually seeking advancement for their sons. Also, they owed their own personal well-being entirely to their royal masters, since everyone else would despise them. Cyrus compared them with gelded horses and bulls: they became tame, yet without losing their capacity for work!

My husband Keith belongs to a mountain rescue team, of which several members are doctors. When I was researching into life at the Persian court, I asked Keith to question one of them about castration and its effects. The doctor told him that the operation would render a man more sensitive, less competitive and aggressive, and less likely to go bald!

'In fact,' he concluded thoughtfully, 'there's really quite a lot to be said for it. . . .'

Actually its effects on the body and the personality depend to a large extent upon how old a boy is when he is castrated, and whether his penis or genitals or both are removed. If you want to know more about the biology or psychology of this intriguing subject, I refer you to *The Harem* by N. M. Penzer, published in 1936 by Harrap and Co. This is an engrossing account of life in the harem of the Turkish sultans by one of the last, and very few, Westerners ever to visit a working oriental harem. The Turkish harem ceased to exist in 1909.

No one should assume that all eunuchs were old and fat with shaven heads, the way they are often shown in illustrations for *The Arabian Nights*. They could be drop-dead gorgeous in earlier life, for only the prettiest boys were chosen for castration. No king wanted ugly specimens decorating his corridors! The operatic 'castrati' of the eighteenth century, male sopranos famous throughout Europe, were so handsome that aristocratic women vied for their affections and swooned at their concerts. Eunuchs can still be found in India: I've never encountered any in the flesh, but I have a fabulous photo of one, taken by the sister of a girl I know. He's the most gorgeous creature you could ever hope to set eyes on.

This is how I have always pictured Hegai, into whose expert care the apprehensive Esther was delivered. Suave and sophisticated as he no doubt was on the outside, inside he must have been traumatized beyond imagining. It's more than likely that he had been gelded as a little boy, perhaps one newly orphaned, amid the smoking ruins of his native Babylon after Xerxes destroyed it. Hegai is a Semitic name, and most probably Babylonian.

What surprises lay in store for the latest addition to

Ahasuerus' burgeoning household? What was harem life really like? As soon as the word 'harem' is mentioned, we tend to picture scenes of sensual self-indulgence in which scantily clad exotic beauties languish contentedly together beside foaming fountains in sun-dappled blossom-filled courtyards devising novel sexual diversions, while cute little page boys wave feathered fans above their heads.

In fact it was probably nothing like this at all. Not only were the girls' rooms pokey and dark (we must remember that the king's women had to be kept out of the sun because white skin was considered far more desirable than a glowing tan, which would make you look like a peasant who had to work in the fields all day) but they probably also hated each other's guts: the jealousy and bitchiness among them would have been indescribable, since they were all competing for the favours of one man. No unmutilated male apart from the king himself was permitted to enter the harem, though occasionally a girl did manage to have an affair with an outsider, for which the penalty was impalement. (Inmates of the Turkish harem used to drop roses through the bars of their windows at the feet of good-looking youths passing below.) There might have been friendship too, but all too often this was tainted by lesbianism as the girls sought relief from acute sexual frustration.

However, it seems that Esther had things easier than most, from the very start. For some reason she found special favour with Hegai (Esther 2:9), as the charm she'd possessed since early childhood now worked its magic even on this urbane palace eunuch. And he must have realized that it would work on the king too, because the way he treats Esther in the biblical text seems to imply that Hegai at least has marked her out for a right royal future. He gives her the best room, and seven maids, in addition to other privileges.

Perhaps it was Hegai rather than Mordecai who gave

Esther her new name, too. As well as being connected with that of the Babylonian goddess Ishtar, Esther means 'star', and the myrtle has star-shaped flowers.

How could Hegai be so sure that the king would like Esther better than her rivals? Did she somehow bear an uncanny resemblance to the deposed Vashti? It seems unlikely that a little Jewish orphan girl could have looked very much like an Aryan queen, but no doubt it was something about her mannerisms and her pride in her own beauty that marked her out, rather than simply her physical characteristics. Then again, it is also very possible that Hegai was considerably better acquainted with the king than a respectable person ought to have been, and thus knew his tastes more intimately than most. There is good evidence to suggest that eunuchs were used sexually by the Persian kings.

And so Esther's twelve months of preparation got under way. Even among more humble Persians, bridal preparations could be surprisingly elaborate, and vestiges of these customs survive in parts of Iran and North India. They include ritual bathing at a communal bath house, the meticulous plucking of the eyebrows and the removal of body hair, the painting of the hands and feet with henna, and the application of striking facial make-up. Paste will already have been applied to the skin over a period of several months, to lighten its colour and texture.

An extended stay on a health farm, or even in a luxury leisure complex, isn't my idea of fun. I must admit I wouldn't want to go to such a place even for a weekend, unless it was lashing down with rain and guaranteed not to stop for the forseeable future. I'd rather be half way up a mountain in the sunshine any day than stuck indoors in a steam bath or have ghastly greases slapped all over my face.

But somehow I imagine that Esther was the kind of girl

who would have enjoyed her months of pampering,
especially once she came to realize that she was regarded as
rather special. Something tells me that she loved the baths
in asses' milk, and the silky feel of the creams that the
slavegirls rubbed into her skin when they had lifted her out
and towelled her dry. She loved the scent of the perfumes
they burned beside her bed at night, which they said would
make her complexion softer and purer than a baby's. She
loved the way they brushed out her hair, and bound it in a
different style each day, according to the latest palace
fashion. More than any of those things in themselves, she
loved being the centre of so many people's attention.

But most of all she loved the smile that lighted Hegai's
face whenever he came to check up on her progress. Just for
a moment the snarl would vanish, along with the sorrow
which she knew it was meant to disguise. She had learned
that the Persians had a word to describe a mythical place of
perfection and beauty; they used it to describe the gardens
with which they liked to surround their houses, too. The
word was 'paradise', and for a season, Esther believed that
she had found it.

It's likely that she became completely assimilated into
Persian courtly life. Nothing is said, in the book which
bears her name, about her eating kosher food or keeping the
sabbath. This is in marked contrast with the case of Daniel
in exile in Babylon, who insisted on a vegetarian diet lest he
unwittingly eat something unclean. If Esther *had* followed
Daniel's example, her Jewishness wouldn't have remained
a secret for very long. Indeed, not only had Esther kept her
Jewishness a secret from others (Esther 2:10), she was probably trying to forget about it herself.

But Hegai wasn't the only person with a keen interest in
how Esther was getting on. Throughout the period of Esther's
preparation, Mordecai 'walked to and fro near the courtyard

of the women to find out how Esther was and what was happening to her' (Esther 2:11). How did he get away with this? Possibly he got himself a post at the palace: we are told that he would 'sit at the king's gate'(Esther 2:19). But even if he did, it's hard to see how he could have got so near the harem. Perhaps there were places where the women could be spied upon: in the Topkapi palace there are spy-holes in some of the walls so that the *women* could find out what the *men* were up to. Maybe it worked both ways. And it seems that Mordecai was a pretty dab hand at spying – a skill he puts to pertinent use later on in the book.

What did he make of what was happening to her? Perhaps he regretted telling her to keep her identity a secret, when he saw how thoroughly Persian she had become. He must have realized that she no longer thought of herself as a Jew even in secret. She had turned her back on her people and their ways. Mordecai was dismayed, for he had let her dead parents down. He feared that he had lost her for ever.

But Mordecai was no more dismayed about Esther than she was about him. Once she became aware that he was watching her every move, her paradise was ruined. For a while she'd been able to put her past behind her; to forget she belonged to a nation that was still in bondage to a foreign potentate, and that she was supposed to be in mourning for the loss of her people's independence. Mordecai's perpetual presence was a thorn in her flesh, a constant reminder of the life – and the God – she'd been happy to turn her back on. But she dared not try to have Hegai remove him, in case awkward questions were asked about her true identity.

At last, in Esther 2:15, the great day arrives. Esther is to go before the king. Each girl was allowed to choose what she wore for this fateful occasion – prospective queens would reveal in the choice they made whether they had good judgement and taste. Yet Esther chooses exactly what

Hegai advises. It appears that she has now become Hegai's puppet just as surely as she had previously been Mordecai's. She is still playing a passive role at this stage in the plot. Things happen to her (2:11) but she does not initiate them.

But then again, I'd say she was sharp enough to realize that Hegai was much more likely to be in sympathy with the king's tastes than she was. Perhaps the other girls decked themselves out gaudily, exciting only revulsion in their royal master, to whom gold and precious stones meant no more than tawdry plastic bangles mean to us. It's only when we have unlimited resources at our disposal that we can demonstrate how magnificently appalling our taste really is! The acquisition of riches is no guarantee that good taste will be acquired to match.

So, this is the moment of truth. Esther has charmed the king's commissioners, and one of his chief eunuchs. But how will the king himself react?

6

Royalty: The Romance and the Reality

Esther sat by the courtyard pool and admired her reflection in the water. Any moment now, the dapper and decorous Hegai would arrive to take her before the king, and she felt ready. Everything was perfect. Her long black hair, thicker and glossier than ever for its twelve months of deep conditioning, was piled into whorls on the top of her head, from which it plunged in shining ringlets all down her back. A delicate blush – part excitement, part rouge – lent a hint of colour to her cheeks, which were creamy and smooth as Egyptian alabaster. The outbreak of spots she had secretly dreaded had not made itself manifest after all, and a sly little smile played on her reddened lips as she thought how horrified Mordecai would be at the sight of her painted eyes, pierced nose and ruthlessly plucked brows if he happened to be spying on her now.

'Well, do you suppose I shall do?' Esther asked of her seven handmaids, who hovered at a respectful distance, their eyes moist with tears as they beheld their mistress's beauty and reflected upon the ordeal that awaited her.

'Do?' repeated the chief of them, all but choking on her words. 'Oh my lady, I never saw Queen Vashti herself look so gorgeous.' And Esther smiled again as she imagined the pleasure that would dance in Hegai's eyes as soon as he caught sight of her.

Poor Hegai. He was going to miss her dreadfully once she had gone from his care. Feared or despised by everyone who encountered him, he had no one but her in all the world whom he could call a friend. Not that she had been a particularly good friend to him either. She knew she had taken him for granted, trying his patience with her extravagant demands, her moods and her sulks, enjoying playing the part of the spoilt little rich girl she had undoubtedly become. Yet he never complained, never gave her the slightest taste of her own bitter medicine. And he was so alluring, so desperately beautiful. What a waste. If only fate had allowed her to meet him in some other place, some other life, where he would not have been robbed of his virility, where they could perhaps have married, and reared sons and daughters as handsome and glamorous as their parents.

It was Hegai himself who raised her from her reverie. He held out one impeccably manicured hand and said, 'Come, Lady Esther. It is time.'

And in that split second, her confidence vanished. No pleasure lighted Hegai's eyes, which were haunted by the spectre of approaching loneliness. In the final glimpse she caught of herself in the pool, she saw lips too full, a nose too Semitic. What if the king should deduce her true origins and grow angry? What if he did not extend the point of his sceptre towards her when she prostrated herself at his feet? Esther had spent enough tedious hours studying the finer points of Persian courtly etiquette to know the precise meaning of any and every gesture the king might make, or not make. And if he chose not to hold out his sceptre to a person who appeared before him, then that person would be led away to die.

But there could be no going back for Esther now. She could not reverse the flow of time and return to being a modest Jewish maid keeping house for her pious cousin. When Hegai leaned forward to drape her veil across her face and she felt the warmth of his breath upon her cheeks, she could only lower her eyes and meekly allow him to lead her into whatever future lay in store for her.

Sitting by the poolside she had relished the thought of Mordecai seeing her in her finery as she was conducted in regal splendour to the Apadana (the audience chamber of the king). She had wished fervently for it to happen. And happen it did, yet without making her feel the way she wanted to feel.

Her cousin was standing alone at a crossroads of corridors as her grand little party swept past, Hegai in the lead and her handmaids bringing up the rear. It seemed that Mordecai had aged ten years in so many days. His face was grey and lined, his back bent. And suddenly Esther saw herself through his faded eyes – not as a beautiful would-be queen, but as a hardened, ungrateful brat, mean-spirited and selfish, who had tossed onto the scrapheap the godly values he had tried to teach her. Lovely on the outside, within she was growing uglier with each passing day, and sooner or later that ugliness would make itself manifest in her countenance just like the crop of spots she had dreaded. Already her eyes were cold in their painted frames.

Meanwhile Mordecai grieved silently, for the pretty, perky little girl he had known, and whose childish will he had tirelessly sought to bend to his own. He grieved for his own failure, and for Esther's dead father, whom he had somehow let down so badly. How could things have gone so horribly wrong? Perhaps he had been too strict, too sombre, too much concerned with the teaching of the Law and too little with communicating to his impressionable ward the joy that is to be found in knowing God. Somehow he had lost his own joy along the way, and had had nothing left to share with the girl except the dry husk of legalism. It was scarcely surprising that she seemed to have turned her back on all that he stood for. It was even less surprising when he recalled instructing her to keep her Jewishness a secret, leaving her little choice but to live in exactly the same way and by the same standards as the Gentiles around her. What a mess he had made of everything.

And so Esther's procession reached its imposing destination. The Apadana had been designed and built to inspire terror in the hearts of all who entered it, and never failed to create the desired effect. Paralysed with dread, Esther stood in its entrance and gazed down its impossible length towards the throne of the king away in the hazy distance. Enormous pillars reared above her head, and the air drifting visibly between them was pungent and smoky with the burning of incense. Two thuribles hung from stands positioned to either side of the platform occupied by the throne; incense was burned in them perpetually whenever the king was present. He was frighteningly present now, awesome indeed in his towering headdress and ankle-length robes of imperial purple.

Only when Hegai took her firmly by the elbow and propelled her forward was Esther able to move at all. Her heart in her mouth and thumping hard enough to make her retch, she walked down the central aisle with what meagre grace she could muster, then sank to the ground like a fallen leaf at the foot of the dais, as custom bade her do, to await the reaction of the king.

Ahasuerus had paid scant attention as the latest specimen had been led in for his approval. Morning by morning they came without relief, one every day, each done up to the nines in frills and flounces, their whitened faces so garishly daubed with paint that they looked little more human than the figures on his friezes. How was an effigy sculpted from ivory and painted like a child's clay doll supposed to keep his bed warm at night? Nevertheless, it was his habit to hold out his sceptre to every one of these unfortunates as a matter of course: while he was heartily sick of the tawdry ritual, he didn't see any reason why its victims deserved to die.

But as his hand moved automatically to extend the sceptre in this new girl's favour, something caused it to falter. It was all he could do not to drop the emblem of his royalty onto the floor. So low was the girl bowed down that he could see nothing whatever of her face, but there was something in the straightness of her back, in the slenderness of her shoulders, and in the way her shining hair fell about her neck that stirred him as only one other woman had ever done. And her clothing! There were no ridiculous frills and flounces, just a simple, elegant gown in deep magenta – Vashti's favourite colour.

He was well aware by this time that the poor creature must be fearing that her final hour had come. Yet now he was actually *afraid* to extend the sceptre, lest when he saw her face it would be just like all the others. He didn't think he would be able to bear the disappointment, which he already felt to be inevitable.

So he was doubly shocked when, without warning or invitation, she suddenly raised her head and looked straight into his eyes. Shocked once, because for a commoner to look at the king without his having granted his express permission was frankly unthinkable in itself, but shocked again, and much more profoundly, because the eyes which met his own were the loveliest he had ever beheld. Yes, they had been embellished with cosmetics, it was true, but so subtly, so skilfully, that their natural beauty was enhanced rather than obscured. And as for the face in which they were set . . . if ever a woman's face could have launched a thousand ships as the Greek story claimed, it must have been a face such as this one. Such symmetry, such harmony, such an irresistible blend of temerity and terror. The girl looked nothing like Vashti whatsoever, and yet he had never in all these four miserable years been so powerfully reminded of her.

*   *   *

In short, Ahasuerus was bowled over by Esther, just as so many lesser men had been before him. I wonder why this was, when she can hardly have been the fair-skinned, blue-blooded Aryan he was expected to be searching for? Perhaps she looked more Aryan than she imagined, more Aryan certainly than the average Jewish girl did. Perhaps the year of skin-lightening treatments had worked exceptionally well. Perhaps there really was something about her which reminded him very powerfully of Vashti. Then again, perhaps, like some high-ranking Nazis during the Second World War, the King of Persia was sexually aroused by that which he claimed to despise.

To me, this latter suggestion seems to have the ring of truth to it. Even if Esther *did* remind the king of Vashti, the fact that he did not enquire too closely into her ethnic background cannot have been a careless oversight on Ahasuerus' part. Provided that he did not *know* that she wasn't an Aryan, then there was no reason why he should not bed her, nor indeed why he should not allow himself to marry her, and allow her to share his throne.

And this is precisely what he did do. That night, as the Great King of Persia took Esther's virginity upon the bed where he had deflowered so many others, he made up his mind that he would take her as his queen as well. . . .

The wedding and coronation duly followed, and a public holiday was declared (Esther 2:18). It may have been a remission of taxes instead, or even a release of prisoners (the Hebrew isn't clear). All are well-attested Persian practices in such circumstances, and all three may well have happened at this juncture – much to the delight of the populace of Shushan. The king also distributed generous gifts to his subjects, and no doubt there were carnivals and parties all across the Persian empire.

But how would the Jewish community in Shushan have reacted to Esther's coronation? Probably with very mixed feelings, ranging from horror to delight.

On the one hand, she had married a 'goy', a Gentile! And the title 'queen' had heavy stigma attached to it in Israel, because Israel didn't rightly have queens, only the wives and mothers of kings. The only women who had been known as 'queen' in Israel's chequered history had appropriated the title for themselves, and had either been foreigners or half-foreign (for example the notorious Jezebel, wife of Ahab, and her daughter Athaliah who set herself up as ruler over Judah) and idol worshippers to boot. For a woman to occupy a throne was seen as a symptom of a disordered society.

Yet on the other hand, the coronation of this comely little orphan girl must have entranced many ordinary Jewish people – not only those who knew of her Saulide connections, but also those for whom she was just an average lass like any other. To think that one of their own had been chosen as the Persian king's new bride! Esther is in fact the only Jewish queen in the Bible who was legitimately entitled to be addressed as such.

In many ways, it must have been rather like Prince Charles marrying Lady Diana Spencer, when she was a shy, innocent kindergarten teacher. Esther was certainly the 'people's princess' of her day. Whether it was possible for such an unlikely marriage to succeed remained to be seen. We're told that Cinderella lived happily ever after with her Prince Charming, but for Esther on the day of her wedding, as for Diana, the problems were only just beginning.

How did the king's associates react to her election? Perhaps many of them, just like Ahasuerus himself, chose to assume that Esther was as Aryan as her royal husband. If not, they kept their opinions to themselves. Conceivably it was better for the king to be married to just about anyone, than pine for Vashti all the time, neglecting to act for the good of his realm while at the same time sowing his seed in other men's furrows.

What about Esther's own feelings concerning the whirl-wind of events in which she found herself caught up? We can only guess, because the text doesn't tell us. I don't suppose that the king or his courtiers meant her to *have* any feelings. She had been uniquely favoured by the richest and most powerful man in the world and would therefore be expected to be content. Perhaps she was. Perhaps she grew to love Ahasuerus as time went by. Perhaps she found him irresistibly attractive from day one, and forgot all about her old friend Hegai, who was left to take out his grief and frustration on the unfortunate girls who remained in his charge, for whom all those elaborate preparations had proven futile. After all, Esther could see that the king was still in the prime of life, and possessed of incredible wealth, authority and sexual experience – a compelling com-bination of attributes in many a young woman's naive and undiscerning eyes.

What then would their married life have been like? We aren't told very much about this either. Presumably Esther lived most of the time in the harem of the concubines, where the king's female relations also lived, but in her own special quarters. It's more than likely that she had the rooms which Vashti had used; I should imagine that this would have made her feel rather uncomfortable. If Vashti could so easily be deposed, how secure was *her* position? What was her role supposed to *be*, as Ahasuerus' wife? No doubt she was hoping to bear the king a son who would sit on the throne of Persia some day. We know that Ahasuerus/Xerxes had had sons already, by his first wife, but there was no law in Persia guaranteeing automatic right of succession to the firstborn. It was up to the king to choose his heir. How extraordinary it would have been if a descendant of Saul had got to be the ruler of the mighty Persian empire. But we don't know if Esther bore the king children or not. If she did not, she must have begun to have serious worries about just how long she would retain the king's favour.

In Chapter 9 we'll be examining Christian attitudes to the role of women as regards leadership within church and society. But one good thing which feminism *has* done is to liberate many women from the assumption that the goal of every woman's life is to bear and nurture children – and from the consequent agony which barrenness used necessarily to bring with it. Of course, there are still women who suffer acute anguish because they want to have children and cannot. But there are others, myself included, who have never wanted children, and see their ministries as lying in other areas.

Recently I was looking for a Christian book on marriage to give to a couple I know whose wedding was imminent. They weren't Christians, but the girl had shown quite a lot of interest in my novels, and in Christianity in general. I found a few books on marriage in my local Christian book-shop, and flicked through them to get a feel for what they had to say. I opened one at random, and found a passage that read: 'A woman who does not bear children is like a ship

which never puts out to sea.' Ugh! The lady running the
shop must have seen me cringe!

For it is the woman (or man) who does not find her or his
purpose in God who is the ship which never goes to sea. It
is right for *some* women to bear children, perhaps most
women. But not all. Likewise it is right for most women to
marry, but not all. For there are vital ministries for single
people and for childless couples which families with
children cannot so readily fulfil. It was the Apostle Paul
who specifically stated that under certain circumstances it is
better to remain single and childless (1 Corinthians 7:8,
25–34), and in making this statement he was only building
on what Jesus himself had taught. In Matthew 19:12 during
a discussion on marriage and divorce Jesus says: 'Some are
eunuchs because they were born that way; others were
made that way by men; and others have renounced marriage
because of the kingdom of heaven.'

In other words, just as Paul based his teaching on that of
Christ, so feminism too is largely built on Jesus' foun-
dations – even though many feminists today may be loath to
admit it! Throughout his ministry Jesus treated women in a
way no other 'respectable' man of his period or part of the
world would have dared to do, welcoming their attention
(Luke 7:36–50), engaging them in conversation in public
places (John 4:1–26), and in every way regarding them as
no less important than men. The Christian gospel itself
treats men and women equally (Galatians 3:28: '. . . there is
neither slave nor free, male nor female'), and the Bible
declares that men and women *together* were made in the
image of God (Genesis 1:27).

It's interesting that in Luke 8:19–21 when Jesus is told
that his mother and brothers are waiting to see him, he
replies, 'My mother and brothers are those who hear God's
word and put it into practice.' These words have two very

startling implications: first, that finding God's will for our lives should take precedence over family concerns, and second that we actually have more in common with those who share our faith than with those who share our genes. This is not the same as saying that we should neglect our children in order to attend a plethora of church meetings! What it *is* saying is that if we don't have any children of our own we are perhaps freer to serve God in the wider world, to share fellowship with other Christians, and to seek to build them up in the faith.

I think that we should probably all seek to have some sort of input into the next generation, but it could take any number of forms. For example, teaching, youthwork, enriching the lives of godchildren or nieces and nephews, fostering, writing children's books, and so on.

Some Christians argue that after the Flood God commanded human beings to 'go forth and multiply' (Genesis 9:7). However, it seems to me this is just about the only biblical injunction that sinful humanity has already carried out to the letter. We certainly *have* filled the earth with our progeny, to the extent that the proliferation of the human race is threatening the survival of many different species with which we are meant to share its resources. We should not forget that in addition to instructing Noah and his family to multiply, God told him to enable all the other species to multiply as well (Genesis 8:17). Perhaps any couple desiring more than two children should seek very specific guidance from God, and there is certainly no reason why any Christian should feel pressurized into getting married or having children at all.

Returning to our heroine, however, it's at this point that an unexpected twist is introduced into her story. . . .

*   *   *

Espionage was hardly a career for which Mordecai had been highly trained. But in the months since Esther had been taken to live at the palace, he had become something of an adept. In all the time she'd been kept in the House of Hegai, scarcely a day had passed without his having managed at least to catch a glimpse of her – taking the air on her balcony in the cool of the evening, sitting by the pool in her courtyard dipping her varnished toes in the water, or strolling with her handmaids or her gelded keeper through the paradise gardens. He had learned to see without being seen, to hear without being heard. And so it was that on one particular day, when Esther had already been queen for some while, Mordecai came to overhear something of infinitely greater significance than he had bargained for.

Bigthana and Teresh were two of the officers who guarded the doorway to the king's private apartments. But they were off duty and skulking in a place they should not have been – as was Mordecai himself – when he heard them conspiring together to murder their royal master in his bed. They were talking head to head in hushed voices, but such was their anger against Ahasuerus that every now and then their words became perfectly audible to Mordecai where he was hiding, and the burden of what they were saying permitted no alternative interpretation.

Mordecai knew that he must act swiftly if the king's life was to be saved and the conspirators exposed. Yet how was he to get his warning across without admitting that he himself had been trespassing where he should not have been? He could only see one way forward, and that was through Esther. Yet how was he, whom everyone at the palace now knew to be Jewish, to make contact with his cousin without giving away the fact that she was Jewish too? For although he had made no secret of his own ethnic background, he had never told any of the colleagues with whom he worked that he was a relative of the new queen.

Once again Mordecai put his undercover skills to good use. He knew that in addition to her handmaids Esther had been assigned a number of the king's eunuchs to attend her. One of these Mordecai intercepted as he went about his errands later that day, drawing him aside into the shadows and telling him everything he had overheard. For Mordecai knew very well that the startled fellow would be obliged to go straight away and report the information to the queen. Which is precisely what the eunuch proceeded to do.

*   *   *

How had Mordecai come to be in a position to overhear this discussion? According to Esther 2:21 it was while he was 'sitting at the king's gate'. This implies that if he hadn't already been given a post at the palace (2:11), he'd almost certainly got one by now. Had Mordecai gained this position through a 'lucky coincidence'? Or had he deliberately engineered it for himself? I'm pretty sure it was the latter – it seems that he was nothing if not resourceful.

So, if Esther had so far been under the impression that royals were somehow guaranteed happiness and security, her illusions would now have been dashed. The life of her husband the king was in grave danger! How would she have felt about this? We aren't told how long the couple had been married when this plot was hatched, nor why it was hatched, except that the two officials 'became angry' (Esther 2:21).

It's interesting to note that when Ahasuerus/Xerxes did eventually die, it was in just such a plot as this. We learn from the historian Ctesias that Xerxes was murdered in a palace plot involving his eunuch chamberlain and the Grand

Vizier. The chamberlain let the assassins into Xerxes' bed-chamber, to slaughter him in his sleep.

Had Mordecai not been in the right place at the right time, then the king might well have been slaughtered a lot sooner! But as things turned out, Esther went straight to her husband and reported to him what her eunuch had told her. The plot was investigated and discovered to be a reality (Esther 2:23); the ringleaders were put to death and Ahasuerus lived to rule another day.

Since Esther expressly gave credit for the plot's discovery to Mordecai, as was his due (Esther 2:22), we might reasonably expect to be told next about his receiving a handsome reward. But no such reward is mentioned, and for a very good reason: because, as we shall find out later, none was given. All that happened in the aftermath of the conspiracy was that the account of the officers' plot was written up in the royal records (2:23). This, incidentally, is another seemingly minor detail which our author delib-erately leaves pending, and which we as readers need to store in our memories.

But *why* was no reward given to Mordecai? Why were honours not heaped upon his head? After all, he had saved the king's life, and with the minimum of adverse publicity; news of the conspiracy may never have leaked beyond the palace walls at all.

It may well have something to do with the fact that Ahasuerus had become much more concerned with hon-ouring another person entirely. For a certain Haman, son of Hammedatha, formerly a junior minister in Ahasuerus' government, had begun a meteoric rise to power of which it seemed the sky was the only limit. Yet Haman was to prove every bit as dangerous an influence as the two rebellious officials whose lifeless bodies now swung on the gallows for the vultures to plunder.

7

A Dire Threat . . .

Haman son of Hammedatha stretched like a leopard and leaned back contentedly against the plush upholstery of his couch. Lacing gem-encrusted fingers behind his head, he surveyed his surroundings with satisfaction.

Who could have guessed, upon entering this sumptuously decorated apartment, that only twelve months ago its occupant had been little better than an office boy? A lowly clerk who had spent his days auditing the imperial accounts in a drab and dirty cupboard. Certainly his quarters had not merited the title 'room' – so small that he could barely open the door to get out.

These days he slept on an ivory bed, in a spacious executive suite with its own balcony, a mere stone's throw from the king's private rooms. In addition he owned a sumptuous house in the city, where he kept his wife and ten sons in the lap of luxury, and with whom he might dine if he so wished. More often than not Haman was invited to dine at the king's table, and to spend the evening with Ahasuerus himself, gaming or drinking. When the king had leisure during the day, the two of them would play polo with the noble lords of Persia, or take part in staged hunts in the paradise gardens.

And it was his own sheer brilliance that had got him where he was today; of that Haman was in no doubt. His

103

sharp eyes and meticulously mathematical mind had helped him spot numerous irregularities in the accounts, and he had exposed several of his venerable colleagues for fraud. Once his genius had been brought to Ahasuerus' attention, and he had been presented to him for special commendation, Haman had set himself the goal of gaining His Majesty's total trust, and had lost no time in attaining it. With catlike dexterity he had sniffed out and tracked down corruption wherever it lurked, everywhere sowing seeds of suspicion until he alone appeared worthy of any man's confidence. As a consequence he had been given more and more responsibility, in return for more and more gold, until just in these past few days his achievements had been crowned with the title of Grand Vizier, First Minister of Persia, making him the most powerful man in the empire excepting Ahasuerus himself.

Not that everyone appreciated his spectacular success story. In particular the king's seven advisors, above whose heads he had been promoted, begrudged him the very air he breathed. Haman was profoundly unconcerned that people hated him; in fact he positively enjoyed seeing the resentment blazing in their eyes. Let them hate me, he thought, so long as they accord me the respect that I deserve.

Which was why he had arranged an audience with the king that very morning and made of him an admittedly unusual but, in Haman's opinion, perfectly reasonable request. Haman desired that whenever any of his subordinates appeared before him, or chanced to cross his path, they should bow down before him just as they did before the king. Somewhat to Haman's surprise, Ahasuerus had granted his request straight away.

It wasn't Ahasuerus' acquiescence in itself that had surprised him, for Haman knew by now that he would always get his way in the end. It was rather the readiness with which the royal consent had been given. Haman had fully expected to have to argue quite forcefully for the legitimacy of his case, and had experienced no little difficulty composing a justification he had thought Ahasuerus might accept. Because he certainly *wouldn't* have accepted the reason paramount in Haman's own mind – that the First Minister was himself of royal blood.

Not *Persian* royal blood, of course. Haman was no more Aryan than the Pharaoh of Egypt. No, he was a descendant of Agag, of the house of the kings of Amalek – kings whose kingdom, alas, existed no more. It had been destroyed long ago, along with most of its population, by its ancestral enemies the people of Israel, whom as a consequence Haman the Agagite had resolved never to forgive. For were it not for that despicable, interfering little nation, he himself would now be sitting not merely upon an upholstered couch, but on a throne!

Suddenly, irked afresh by this troublesome thought, Haman sprang up and strode indignantly across the room. He flung open the lattice doors which led to his balcony and stepped outside into the warm spring day. At once the courtiers going about their business in the yard below fell to their knees, as the king's new decree required them to do whenever his Grand Vizier appeared, and Haman began to feel rather better once again.

Then he noticed that in the far corner of the yard there was one elderly man who remained stolidly on his feet.

Haman was incensed. For while it was faintly conceivable that the decrepit old greybeard had not seen him emerge, it was utterly beyond belief that he could have failed to observe his comrades falling on their knees like skittles all around him.

Marching back inside his apartment, Haman bellowed for his slaves, who came at the double as they always did, lest tardiness earn them a beating.

'Fetch that doddering old dunderhead to me!' Haman roared. 'Fetch him here this minute!' And the finger with which he pointed in the old man's direction was visibly quaking with rage. His two most senior slaves ran out onto the balcony to identify the felon in question, but could not for the life of them see who their master meant.

'The only man standing up, you imbeciles!' thundered Haman, thrusting them aside and boxing their ears as he did so.

But when he reached the balustrade and looked out into the yard, the aged recalcitrant was nowhere to be seen.

*   *   *

The book of Esther first introduces us to Haman at the beginning of its third chapter. Here we are told that he has been appointed to the highest office in the land; in other words he has been promoted above the heads of everyone else at court. Indeed, it's possible that the office of Grand Vizier was actually created for him. It isn't clear *when* this happened, the text just says 'after these events' (Esther 3:1), but the next date we are given is Ahasuerus' twelfth regnal year (3:7), so it must have been before this. Esther and Ahasuerus have now been married for quite some time, and still, so far as we know, Esther has borne no son.

Haman's ancestry is highly significant. We are told that he is an Agagite, which almost certainly means that he was a descendant of Agag, King of Amalek, who had been a contemporary of Esther and Mordecai's ancestor King Saul and had fought against him in battle (see 1 Samuel 15). Saul had defeated him, but let him live when he had been commanded by God to put him to death. In the end Samuel had done the deed for him, but Agag must have had sons already who lived to pass on their father's name.

The Amalekites had actually been enemies of Israel since the time of the exodus from Egypt. The story of this enmity is told in Exodus 17:8–16, Deuteronomy 25:17–19 and 1 Samuel 15. It all began when the Amalekites made an unprovoked attack upon the Israelites as they escaped through the wilderness with Moses. After the Amalekite army was defeated, God told Moses that he would 'completely erase the memory of the Amalekites from under heaven'. In Deuteronomy the Israelites are reminded of this, and told that when they enter the Promised Land and have rest from all their enemies, they must ensure that Amalek is destroyed. In 1 Samuel, Saul is challenged by God to carry out this command, since it still hasn't been done: he must spare neither men nor women, children nor animals. Saul defeats the Amalekites comprehensively, but keeps the best animals and takes the king, Agag, alive. When Samuel calls him to account, Saul claims that he's kept the animals in order to sacrifice them to God, but Samuel says that God demands obedience, not sacrifice, and has therefore rejected Saul as king. Samuel himself then puts Agag to death.

Obedience, not sacrifice . . . what an important biblical principle this is. It runs through so much of the Old Testament, and the New Testament as well, yet it is so rarely recognized or fully understood. It's all too common among Christians for puritanical piety to take the place of a vibrant relationship with God. Of course, this trend has been more prevalent in some periods, places and denominations than in others. Watching TV, going to the cinema, dancing, drinking and the like have all been outlawed by various churches at various times, presumably because they might involve fun or excitement of some kind. But God is not a celestial spoilsport who expects us to give up the things we enjoy, just because we enjoy them! What he does expect is that we will listen to him and do what he tells us to do. This may involve giving things up, but it may not. What it certainly will involve is fun and excitement. I'm reminded of the young Jackie Pullinger's reaction in *Chasing the Dragon* when a clergyman friend suggested to her that if she wanted to know which part of the world God was calling her to, she should get on a boat going as far as she could afford to go, and pray to know when to get off! She said, 'But that can't be right. It would be fun!'

Going back to Esther, you might well be wondering why, if the author wants us to pick up on the connections between her story and Saul's, he doesn't make them clearer. It's probably because to those readers who knew their Jewish history, they would be blindingly obvious – and to those who didn't, they would be quite meaningless anyway, so there was no point in labouring them.

To those readers who did know their history, a clash between Mordecai and Haman would seem inevitable. And it wouldn't merely be a clash of personalities, but the climax of a feud hundreds of years old, involving not only Mordecai and Haman as individuals, but the families and nations from which they came.

We have already observed that throughout the book of Esther, God seems to be strangely conspicuous by his absence. But in Esther chapter 3 the same is true of Esther herself! Just as in a soap opera, the focus of the action has shifted temporarily to other characters in the story, and follows the conflict between Mordecai and Haman as it develops, while Esther remains blissfully unaware of the storm that is building around them. It is only in chapter 4 that one of her handmaids alerts her to what is going on. . . .

*   *   *

As soon as Haman received his spectacular promotion, Mordecai knew it spelt Trouble with a capital T. It wasn't only the fact that Haman was an Amalekite. It was the personality of the man himself. Haman was one of the most arrogant and avaricious individuals Mordecai had ever had the misfortune to encounter. Employing shameless self-publicity and the most brazen flattery of the royal personage, he had insinuated himself into the king's affections, amassing for himself more and more privileges and responsibilities with every day that passed. At first Mordecai found it almost impossible to believe that Ahasuerus couldn't see through this upstart's slimy scheming, but then he reflected that the king never *had* been a very shrewd judge of character. After all, he had allowed his recklessly ambitious cousin Mardonius to bamboozle him into a protracted war in Greece, without ever seeing that Mardonius cared nothing for the good of Persia or its people, and everything for his own political advancement. Haman was tarred with precisely the same brush, and now Ahasuerus was making the same mistake again. What the implications would be for his unfortunate subjects scarcely bore thinking about.

So now Haman was the imperial favourite, and he knew it, strutting about the palace like one of the peacocks in the paradise gardens. Yet he would not be fully satisfied until everyone else knew it too. This was why he had taken it into his head to demand that every person resident or employed at the palace, with the exception of Ahasuerus himself, should 'kneel down and pay him honour'. And, incredibly, everyone was doing so, much as they may have resented it, except for Mordecai.

'Why don't you just do as he wants?' his colleagues

reproached him. 'Don't make a mountain out of a molehill.
We're always having to bow and scrape to someone in this
place. Why not bow to Haman too? It's no big deal.'

*   *   *

They had a point. Courtly etiquette involved a great deal of
bowing and scraping. There were detailed regulations
governing just who had to bow and scrape to whom, and in
what way: whether they were to bow down low or simply
incline the head or touch the forelock; whether they were to
kiss a superior on one cheek or both, or on the hand; and so
on. Mordecai must have had to bow the knee before a
plethora of people every day of his life, and if he appeared
before the king he would have been required to perform a
full prostration, spreadeagled on the ground. Yet we don't
hear of Mordecai having a problem with any of this. Indeed,
bowing before others was a feature of Jewish culture too.
Suppliants might bow when seeking favour (Genesis 33:3)
or showing indebtedness (1 Samuel 20:41).

So why did Mordecai take such exception to bowing
before Haman in particular? The only reason given in the
text is that he was a Jew, but this in itself doesn't answer the
question. What answer would he have given to those who
considered his attitude odd? I think that there would have
been several strands to Mordecai's argument. First of all,
bowing signified respect, and Mordecai could see quite
clearly that Haman was worthy of no respect whatsoever. It
would have been frankly hypocritical of Morcedai to accord
respect to someone he recognized as a dangerous manipulator who was exerting a pernicious influence over the king.
It's very likely that Mordecai already felt that he had let

God down in his raising of Esther, and he was determined
not to let him down again now. 'If we bow before Haman,
a quiet life is the last thing we can expect,' Mordecai would
have pointed out. 'If we let him have his way in a matter
such as this today, what will he demand of us tomorrow? If
only you, my colleagues, would offer me your support
instead of your criticism, we might be able to stop him
before it's too late.'

And he would have had a point, too. How much evil
could have been averted down the ages if the many had
made a stand against the few? Yet fear for themselves and
for their families, and suspicion of their neighbours, has all
too often caused the many to stick their heads in the sand
while men like Hitler and Stalin – and Haman – have risen
inexorably to supreme power, and their repressive regimes
have led to unimaginable suffering for huge numbers of
people. We ourselves may never be called upon to make a
stand against evil on this kind of scale, when the stakes are
so high – at least, let's pray that we won't. Yet we face
similar situations frequently in the workplace or school,
among our neighbours, or even in the church. Do we 'mind
our own business' when bullying or vandalism, corruption,
sexual immorality or exploitation are poisoning the
relationships of those around us? Are we more afraid of
laying our jobs or our friendships on the line than we are of
asking God what we ought to be doing to put things right?
The old adage is true: if we're not part of the solution, we're
only adding to the problem.

The second strand to Mordecai's argument may have
been simply that Haman was an Agagite, and therefore he
could not permit himself to bow down before a man who
belonged to a family and a race that continued to cling onto
existence only because God's servants had failed to carry
out a divine injunction to the letter.

The remaining strands to the argument are a little more complex, and relate to what this 'bowing' before Haman actually signified in the latter's eyes. It seems he was demanding something that was not merely a straightforward sign of respect, but much more like the obeisance due to the king. We know that he had serious delusions of grandeur – in Esther chapter 6 he fantasizes about wearing one of the king's robes and riding His Majesty's horse through the streets of Shushan. If he was demanding actual prostration, it's little wonder that Mordecai could not bring himself to acquiesce. For Persians and Semites viewed prostration rather differently. To a Persian it signified respect for a king, his regent or equivalent, but to a Semite, prostration was connected with the worship of a god. Mordecai no doubt felt that to bow before a Semite compromised his faith in a way that bowing before a Persian did not. Persian kings regarded themselves as agents of Ahura-Mazda, but not as divine in their own right (unlike the Egyptian pharaohs, for example). In other words, Mordecai imagines that being a king wouldn't be enough for Haman; he'd really like to be deified!

But, like Vashti, Mordecai must surely have understood that adhering so rigidly to his principles in this way could have very dangerous consequences, and not only for himself. It has been suggested that Mordecai set out deliberately to provoke Haman, in order to bring the centuries-old feud between Israel and the remnant of Amalek to a conclusive end.

And it very nearly meant the conclusive end of the Jewish people. For Haman, enraged by Mordecai's refusal to toe the line, resolved upon the destruction of every Jew resident in Ahasuerus' domains (Esther 3:6).

Of course, this represents a punishment out of all proportion to the crime, but not as far as Haman was concerned. He had come to believe his own publicity to such an extent that in his opinion there could be no crime more serious than attempting to undermine the authority of the king's favourite. Moreover, Haman hated the Jews already, and an excuse to destroy them was precisely what he had been looking for. He must have realized, too, that Mordecai would not be cowed into submission by any kind of threat to himself, but a threat to his people was a different matter.

So Haman decides to cast lots in order to determine an auspicious day for the destruction to take place (Esther 3:7). We should note that he does this *before* saying anything about it to the king. He knows that the king will go along with what he is planning, so long as he handles him skilfully.

This is the first time that the book connects itself expressly with the festival of Purim. The word used for 'lot' is *pur*, which is not the usual Hebrew word, but archaeologists have found an Assyrian die inscribed with the word *puru*.

The practice of casting lots to determine lucky days for important events was well established in Persia. The Persians, like the Assyrians, believed firmly in predetermined fate, with which it was important to co-operate if their enterprises were to be successful.

And so we have returned to the theme of luck, or fate versus destiny. As we have said (in Chapter 3), the real challenge for us as Christians is to rise above our 'fate', breaking down the barriers of background and circumstance with which Satan would seek to limit our effectiveness, in order to fulfil the destiny that God has prepared for us. In Christ we can conquer fate just as we can conquer death. It's true that we're not all born equal: some of us have a much tougher struggle than others, perhaps because we have come from dysfunctional homes, or have had little education, or inherited the wrong genes! But didn't the

Apostle Paul write: 'Not many of you were wise by human standards; not many were influential; not many were of noble birth' (1 Corinthians 1:26)? It is pointless to blame parents or poverty or our star sign or anything else, if we don't achieve what God is calling us to do. Once we have given our lives to Christ, we have been reborn and these things should no longer have a hold over us. If they do, then perhaps we need to seek counselling or deliverance; but, more importantly, we need to seek God. He doesn't want second best for any of us.

Haman's 'auspicious day' turns out to be a whole year away! He casts the lots during Nisan, the first month of the year, whereas Adar, the month in which the fateful day falls, is the twelfth. So the Jews were going to have to spend a whole year with a death sentence hanging over them.

Still, at least this meant that God would have more opportunity to intervene. Or at least it would seem that way to his terrified people. No doubt God could have intervened just as effectively if the auspicious day had only been a week away. It might just have been harder for the Jews to believe that he could.

Once Haman has hit upon his lucky day he goes to the king and tells him what he is intending to do – except that he doesn't really tell him at all. He tells him half-truths, which are no different from lies. He warns him that imperial security is threatened by 'a certain people dispersed and scattered' throughout the empire.

With this phrase he implies that their subversive influence is everywhere, and he deliberately avoids giving the *name* of the people. This is because Ahasuerus would certainly have known about the Jews, and that what Haman was saying about them was not true. Haman therefore pretends that the people to whom he is referring belong to some obscure sect which can quite easily be stamped out so long as it is done soon.

Haman strengthens his case by playing on the king's paranoia. The people he wishes to destroy aren't merely 'scattered', but they keep themselves separate. Their customs are 'different from those of all other people' and they 'do not obey the king's laws' (Esther 3:8). This last statement is a downright lie on Haman's part. In fact the Jews probably kept their own laws in *addition* to Persian laws, but since subject peoples were at liberty to keep any additional laws they chose, it was no good Haman criticizing them for doing it. (Each province had two courts, one to enforce its own laws, and one for those of the Persians.) Haman had to make the king think that the Jews kept their own laws to the exclusion of Persia's. He summarizes his case by claiming that it's not 'in the king's best interests to tolerate them'(3:8).

Haman finally promises to put ten thousand talents (a truly stupendous sum) in the royal treasury, possibly from his own pocket, though more likely he means to confiscate the Jews' property and give it to the king. There was no distinction between the state coffers and the king's private purse. In theory *everything* belonged to the king, just as did *everyone*. This is the essence of Persian feudalism: all the king's subjects were his slaves, and all their land and property was in effect leased to them by him.

The king falls for Haman's scheming, hook, line and sinker. He doesn't merely agree to Haman's plan, he actually hands over his signet ring, thereby enabling Haman to issue any edict he thinks fit and stamp it, literally, with the royal seal of approval. In effect, he abdicates all his power – to a non-Aryan upstart! And he tells him to keep the money. No doubt he is so grateful to Haman for having the foresight to liquidate this dangerous element before it's too late, that he is prepared to make Haman a good deal richer than he already is.

Ahasuerus has quite clearly been manipulated by Haman, just as he was manipulated by his seven advisors earlier on. (We aren't told what has become of them – Haman has utterly stolen their limelight.) How right the king's uncle Artabanus was when he said, according to Herodotus, 'My lord, you are led astray by the companionship of bad men.' The better we get to know them, the more Herodotus' Xerxes and the book of Esther's Ahasuerus come across as one and the same person.

The edict against the Jews is drawn up – by Haman. It is written out by the royal secretaries in the script of each province and the language of every subject people. By including this detail in his account, the author of 'Esther' once again demonstrates his familiarity with Persian custom, for Persian inscriptions too are always multilingual. The edict is sent to the satraps (governors of the 20 satrapies, i.e. the administrative regions of the empire) and their subordinates (governors of each individual province within the satrapies), and also to the provincial aristocracies. Although Haman drafts the document, it is sealed with Ahasuerus' seal and goes out in his name.

It is significant that the day the edict goes out, 13th Nisan (Esther 3:12) is the day before the slaying of the Passover lambs (see Exodus 12:6). The imminence of the Passover celebrations, commemorating the exodus of the Jewish slaves from Egypt under Moses, could hardly fail to make the Jews throughout the Persian empire think, 'God saved us then; can't he do it now?' This constituted a real test of faith. How desperately the Persian Jews must have pleaded with God for their own lives, when they took the lives of those lambs!

Sometimes such desperation can be a good thing, however. Somehow it's when we're at our most desperate that we truly feel our prayers are getting through. When I was at university and wretchedly unhappy, it was at the times when I said to God, 'Unless something happens today, I'm leaving,' that friends would call unexpectedly and take me out, or I would receive an encouraging letter or some piece of really good news. I'm sure it ought not to be the case that we have to be at the point of gnawing our legs off before God succeeds in convincing us that he's there after all! But I'm also sure that the more earnestly we seek God, the more swiftly he will find us. Perhaps one of the reasons why we don't see more of our family and friends converted is that we just aren't desperate enough for them to come to know God. Repeating formulae (Lord, please speak to Uncle Fred and Auntie Flo . . .) is not real prayer. What prayer *is*, we'll see more clearly in due course.

The Greek version of 'Esther' claims to give us the actual wording of the edict Haman issued. In addition to incorporating 'God' fifty times into the story, the Greek version of 'Esther' contains five substantial additions altogether.

1. An introduction, which includes a dream dreamt by Mordecai in which he sees two dragons fighting. It's there to make sure we realize the cosmic nature of the struggle between himself and Haman.
2. The edict.
3. Prayers of Mordecai and Esther on the Jews' behalf, intended to strengthen the book's religious emphasis.
4. Esther's approach to the king.
5. Mordecai's interpretation of his dream.

When Jerome produced a revised Latin version of the Old Testament in the fourth century AD he relegated these passages to a collection of secondary writings we know as the Apocrypha, because they were not found in the original

Hebrew and were probably written much later.

The edict contains the order to 'destroy, kill and annihilate all the Jews . . . and to plunder their goods' (Esther 3:13). Destroy, kill, annihilate . . . this reads just like a legal document of today, full of seemingly tautologous jargon so that every conceivable interpretation and shade of meaning is accounted for. In the world of bureaucracy little changes except the technology used to record it all. There can be no doubt whatsoever as to the meaning of this particular document! The destruction is to take place on a single day, the 13th of Adar.

Mounted couriers sped away with copies of Haman's document. (No Persian would walk when he could ride.) This was the method habitually used by the Persian kings to disseminate information. Royal roads, paved where necessary, were kept open in all weathers when at all possible, and bandits were rigorously kept at bay. A caravan took 90 days to travel from Susa to Sardis; royal couriers could do it in a week. Archaeologists have found a courier's leather bag containing official letters with names and addresses and a summary of contents on the outside of each.

Meanwhile the king and Haman sat down to have a celebratory drink, though outside the palace, the citizens of Shushan were horrified and bewildered. This was because Persian law was famous for being strict, but fair. This kind of brutality just wasn't what the inhabitants of the Achaemenid empire were used to. Persia was not a corrupt oriental autocracy. Judicial corruption was treated very seriously. Under King Cambyses a judge was executed for taking a bribe – and his skin was used to make a new cover for the judgement seat!

Another thing which is not clear from the text is who exactly is to carry out the imperial orders. We aren't told anything to indicate that imperial troops would carry them out. It sounds more as though ordinary civilians must rise up and kill their Jewish neighbours. Some historians have maintained that this, like the beauty contest, is totally unrealistic. However, in Herodotus there is a very similar scenario. A certain magus known as Gaumata or 'Pseudo-Smerdis' usurped the throne of Persia. When he was deposed, an order was given that on a certain day all magi were entitled to be slaughtered, by whoever! Only nightfall prevented the entire caste from being wiped out. An annual festival was then instituted; on one day every year no magus was allowed to show himself out of doors.

The magi were a fearsome bunch, and we can well understand why people might have wanted to slaughter them! But why would anyone want to slaughter the Jews? How could ordinary people be expected to do this sort of thing?

I can only say that ordinary people have been induced to commit equally horrific crimes throughout history. We need look no further than the last decade of the twentieth century. Rwanda, Bosnia, Kosovo and Indonesia all bear witness to the 'ordinary' people who have taken an active part in repression, persecution and murder. Sometimes we look at our non-Christian friends and reflect upon how nice they are, causing us to question what we're supposed to believe about the fall of man. But human nature is fatally flawed, and, given the circumstances, will show itself as such.

Presumably Ahasuerus wasn't the only anti-Semite. And although Haman's race was Semitic as well, in many folks' minds 'Semitic' meant 'Jewish' just as it does today. Possibly Haman suspected he would fall from favour one day due to his non-Aryan background, and he wanted to channel Ahasuerus' anti-Semitism into hatred of only one group of Semites in particular. Probably there was already resentment of the Jews in many quarters. The Persian empire was weakening, along with its economy. The failure of the

Greek expedition had so encouraged the Greeks that they had become the aggressors and begun to take cities and islands from Persia. A scapegoat was needed for Persia's problems; many of the Jewish exiles had no doubt done comparatively well for themselves, and their success was resented, as it has been down the ages. Haman probably needed to do little other than exploit an animosity which existed already.

So genocide was on the cards – or 'ethnic cleansing', call it what you will – and the author of 'Esther' clearly intends his readers to be utterly shocked by the prospect. But is it so very different from what the Israelites themselves were commanded to do to the Canaanites who had taken possession of the Promised Land while Israel was captive in Egypt? Many readers of Scripture have enormous difficulty with God's instruction that all these people were to be wiped out; it looks all too similar to what the whites tried to do to the Native Americans or the Aborigines in Australia.

This is a very difficult issue, but times and situations change. What is right in one set of circumstances is not automatically justifiable in another. The return of the Jews to Canaan after their period of slavery in Egypt was a unique event in history, and because of the prevalence of idolatry in the land to which they were returning, the very survival of true religion was at stake.

However, it is not our job to apologize for the conduct of the Creator! Mercy is a virtue, but not necessarily to be applied in every circumstance. When grappling with difficult passages in the Old Testament we would do well to remember the dictum 'Do not seek to be more righteous than God'.

8

. . . A Desperate Dilemma

When Mordecai first learned of Haman's edict against the Jews, he could not believe what he was hearing.

'You must be mistaken,' he told the errand boy who had rushed to bring him the news. 'His Majesty would never sanction such an outrage.' Yet even before the words had escaped his lips, Mordecai felt a cold wave of nausea sweep over him, and fear settled like a dead weight in the pit of his stomach. The boy spoke the truth, and he knew it. The web of evil which Haman had been spinning around the Persian king was complete; Ahasuerus was fully enmeshed. The empire was no longer ruled by a tolerant Achaemenid monarch, but by an Amalekite schemer who would not rest until his enemies were destroyed – not only his personal enemies, but the ancestral enemies of his people.

Mortified and despairing, the queen's cousin tore his garments, clothed himself in sackcloth and smeared his brow with ashes. Then out he went into the streets of Shushan, weeping and wailing like a man possessed.

He hadn't set out to go to the palace. In fact he hadn't set out to go anywhere in particular, because he was in no fit state to think rationally about doing anything at all. His tears prevented him from seeing very much more than the ground at his feet, and the bitterness of his crying meant that he couldn't hear the shouts of the muleteers, into the paths of whose animals he was heedlessly stepping. He didn't even notice the crowds of people who stood and stared at him as he plied up and down the alleyways scooping up dust from the gutters and rubbing it into his hair.

But they certainly noticed him. Some of them actually recognized him as the placid, dignified old rabbi who had painstakingly taught their sons the Hebrew scriptures. Whatever could have happened to cause him to carry on like this? Had the poor fellow gone mad?

Anyhow, it was at the palace gates that Mordecai ended up, and it was here that he was prevented from going any further. His way was barred by armed guardsmen who, although they knew perfectly well who he was, crossed their spears and would not let him pass.

'You know the rules, sir,' they reminded him. 'No one dressed for mourning is allowed to enter the royal precincts.'

So Mordecai just sat down where he was by the gateway, in the midst of the lepers and the flea-ridden beggars who sat there all the time craving alms from those who went by. There he gave himself up to his grief, not caring what deadly sickness he might catch from the wretches surrounding him. From earliest infancy he had done his best to honour God, and this was where his dedication had got him. It seemed to him that the Lord had taken his devotion and his loyalty and thrown them back in his face.

Eventually one of the lepers crawled right up beside him and thrust his own disfigured face into Mordecai's. 'You don't belong with the likes of us,' the creature growled, clawing at Mordecai's neatly trimmed beard with what little remained of his fingers. 'What are you doing here, mister? A gentleman such as yourself, grovelling in the gutter with the scum of the earth?'

So Mordecai told him, when he was able, in between

bouts of sobbing and cries of rage against God, against Haman and the world.

Thus gradually the truth got out, spreading from the beggars to the guards, and from the guards to the itinerant merchants and the civil servants who came and went on palace business. By the time the official proclamation concerning the fate of the Jews was made aloud in the city square, most of the population already knew what was coming, and Mordecai was by no means the only august Jewish gentleman clad in sackcloth and ashes.

However, as happens so often in affairs of this kind, those who should have been the first to find out what was going on were the last. While the city reeled with shock, Esther and her attendants were blithely pursuing their domestic routine quite unaware that anything was wrong.

*   *   *

It's at the beginning of Esther chapter 4 that we learn of Mordecai's reaction to Haman's 'final solution'. We witness him going out into the city 'wailing loudly and bitterly' (4:1); and well he might, because in a very real sense the impending catastrophe was all his fault. It was a catastrophe of incalculable significance, threatening not only the lives of many thousands of individuals, but the very survival of God's people. For Judah was as much a part of Ahasuerus' empire as Shushan was.

Mordecai's public show of anguish contrasts sharply with the cool complacency of Ahasuerus and Haman who sat carousing together in the palace. It might even be considered by some modern readers to have been 'over the top' – perhaps deliberately so, as though he were engaging in a theatrical ploy calculated to attract Esther's attention. Conceivably he was. However, we should bear in mind that public grief was perfectly normal, not just in Jewish culture but among the Persians too, as indeed it still is in many parts of the world. Herodotus tells us that the Persians tore their clothes after their fleet was defeated by the Greeks at Salamis. Even today many Jews in the West make a small tear in their clothing when mourning the dead.

Did the Jews themselves blame Mordecai for what was going to happen to them? Probably many of them did, in just the same way that their forefathers blamed Moses after his initial efforts to free them from slavery had failed. Because of the trouble Moses had caused, the Pharaoh made the slaves produce their daily quota of bricks without any longer being given the straw for doing so (Exodus 5).

Did Mordecai in turn blame God? I know I might very well have done so! I might have said, 'Lord, I stuck my neck out for you, and this is how you've rewarded me! And all these years I've been praying for the welfare of your people in exile . . . is *this* the place to which my faithfulness has brought them?'

Actually, I don't really mean that I *might* do this. Let's be honest: I *have* done it! Because this sort of thing so often happens to us all, albeit on a smaller scale. When Keith and I were involved in running an Alpha course at our home some time ago, no end of things would go wrong on a Tuesday evening each week just before it was due to start. Local children would ring the doorbell and run off, or hammer on our windows. Friends would phone up in desperate straits wanting us to sort out whatever crises they were facing. Once, we'd been cutting the hedge, and Keith came out in a horrendously itchy rash – he'd never had anything remotely like it before! As soon as we lift our heads above the trenches, spiritually speaking, Satan tries to shoot us down! It's only when we're muddling along ineffectually that he leaves us alone. He's longing for us to say to God, 'Well, that's the last time I do anything for *you*,' or for us to start doubting that God loves us, or that he even exists at all.

Not that many of us in Britain today can ever have found ourselves in straits as dire as Mordecai's, where the very lives of ourselves and our loved ones have been under threat on account of our standing up for our principles. Before we put other people at risk we should always ask ourselves whether the principle at stake is actually worth standing up for, because it may well not be, as we saw back in Chapter 3. I hope that Mordecai had prayerfully considered the implications of his stance beforehand, or else he might well have felt like we do sometimes, when we've acted from the best of intentions but everything seems to have gone pear-shaped! Already painfully aware of his failure to bring Esther up in the way her parents would have wished, it seemed now that he might finish up being responsible for the total demise of the Chosen People. We must never *assume* that we know God's will. If Mordecai was convinced that he had done the right thing, all he could cling to now was the hope that this fiasco had been allowed to come about so that through it God might be glorified in some way.

At this point in the narrative, Esther herself comes under the spotlight once more . . .

*   *   *

It was the chief handmaid who first informed her of Mordecai's disturbing behaviour.

'Excuse me, my lady,' the girl said, bobbing in a curtsey as she entered, 'but you know that Jewish businessman who keeps coming here wanting to see you? The one who's owed money by your father? Well they say he's been outside the palace gates all morning, my lady, and he's been behaving very strangely. The guards won't let him inside.'

Esther said nothing at first in response, though she felt her heart begin to race. She knew exactly who the slave girl was talking about, for the story she had come out with was the one that Esther had told to all her handmaids and eunuchs in order to explain Mordecai's habitual loitering in the vicinity of her apartments. Lately he had grown bolder, and was constantly approaching one or another of her servants craving permission to speak with their royal mistress, but always she had refused.

What she had really wanted to tell them was that he was undoubtedly some demonized fanatic with a dangerous fixation upon her, and would someone please have him removed forthwith.

But this would never have worked, because by now Mordecai had become a highly respected member of the royal establishment. Attempting to have him prosecuted for stalking would only have attracted a good deal of unwelcome attention regarding the nature of their relationship, and would have certainly led to Esther's Jewish identity being discovered.

'Well,' she said eventually, fanning herself with affected nonchalance and popping a honeyed date into her mouth, 'I would sooner have him outside the palace gates than within. But I fail to see why he should have been refused entry today, when on every other day he gets to wander at will through my husband's courts.'

'My lady, it's as I said: he's not acting like himself. And he's clad in sackcloth like a hired mourner, when he must know he'll never be granted entry dressed like that.'

Esther's heart raced even faster. For she couldn't think of a single individual whose death might have affected Mordecai so powerfully. The kinswoman who had taken her to Vashti's banquet and helped her pack her things for the palace had long since passed away, and they no longer had any surviving relatives whatever. Esther and her cousin were all that remained of the royal house of Saul.

'My lady, do you not think we should send someone to him to find out what is the matter?' the girl suggested, curtseying again lest her mistress suppose she was being presumptuous.

'I think we should ignore him completely as we always do, and hope that he goes away, as he always does in the end,' Esther replied, biting into another date and lazily licking the honey from her fingertips.

'But my lady, you have not seen him,' ventured a second of her handmaids, one who rarely spoke at all, let alone in contradiction of her queen. Behind her, the rest of Esther's slavegirls and eunuchs nodded in goggle-eyed confirmation, and another added, 'My lady, he's been trailing up and down howling like a ghost from the marshes. And he's covered in dust and filth. What do you suppose it can mean?'

'I couldn't be less interested in what it means,' retorted Esther, leaping to her feet at last. 'But if it concerns you all so profoundly, then for heaven's sake one of you take him some decent clothes to put on. And be quick about it.'

*   *   *

Why did Esther react in this way (Esther 4:4)? Could she have seriously thought that Mordecai was wearing filthy sackcloth out of necessity, because some material loss had robbed him even of the clothes he was standing up in?

Perhaps she was just trying to encourage him to come in off the street and explain himself to someone, since apparently no one wearing sackcloth was allowed to enter the palace precincts (Esther 4:2). This regulation isn't attested anywhere else, but is perfectly in keeping with the way Persian protocol operated. Presumably the Persian king was not supposed to be reminded of disaster by having mourning going on within his gates – and in Ahasuerus'/ Xerxes' case there were plenty of disasters for him to remember all too well.

But I think it more probable that she was acutely embarrassed by the scene Mordecai was making and was horribly afraid that somehow he was going to get her into trouble by drawing attention to himself in this way, even though she could have had no inkling as yet of just how serious that trouble might be. The NIV tells us that Esther was 'in great distress' over Mordecai's behaviour; the Talmud helpfully informs us that the Hebrew phrase used is actually a polite way of saying that 'her bowels were loosened'!

So in Esther 4:4 the decent clothes are duly dispatched, but Mordecai refuses to accept them. Esther is left with little choice but to send one of her eunuchs, Hathach, to speak directly to Mordecai and find out what exactly is going on. Mordecai tells him, in detail, even giving him a copy of the edict, which Hathach is to show and explain to Esther in case she doesn't believe him. Mordecai's objective in doing all this is to persuade Esther to go to the king and plead for her people.

It isn't clear whether at this stage he thinks she can do this without at last revealing the secret of her own birth. Perhaps he imagines she can get away with craving mercy for the 'certain people dispersed and scattered' (Esther 3:8) without necessarily confessing that she is one of them. Of course, once she has heard about the edict, Esther is likely to be more desperate than ever to keep her nationality a secret.

Esther is now faced with an agonizing dilemma. But her immediate problem isn't so much that Ahasuerus may guess that she herself belongs to the proscribed sect. (By now Ahasuerus must in fact have known that this sect was to be identified with the Jews, but the edict against them had already been published, so it was too late for him to thwart Haman's plan.) The problem is getting to see the king at all.

For at this juncture we learn that, whatever Esther's marriage was like in its early stages, things now are far from well. It isn't a matter of her softening up her hubby with some sweet nothings on the sofa and then popping her question on the Jews' behalf. The king has not 'sent for her' (i.e. chosen to spend the night with her) for 30 days.

Why should this be? We are not told, but clearly for some reason Esther had fallen seriously out of favour. Perhaps it was because she had borne the king no son; perhaps he had grown tired of her; perhaps he was missing Vashti, and knew that no matter how much Esther might remind him of her, she could never fully take the place of the one true love of his life whom he had lost on account of his own foolish behaviour.

Whatever the cause of the couple's alienation, it must have been a grave one. For Esther recalls, and is seriously worried by, the fact that no man or woman is permitted to go before the king without being summoned, on pain of death.

Like all heads of state, the Persian king was surrounded by tight security, both to protect him from attempts upon his life, and to prevent him being continually vexed by petty requests. He gave audiences at his own discretion, by personal invitation. Herodotus tells us that the Median King Deioces, whose kingdom had subsequently been fused with that of Persia, had introduced the ceremonial which severely restricted access to the king's presence. If you entered without invitation, your life would be forfeit. Only if the king condescended to extend the tip of his golden sceptre towards you would your life be spared; and it seems that Esther was by no means confident that he would do this for her.

Why couldn't Esther have simply requested an audience with the king through the usual channels? Although access was severely restricted, there were designated procedures for requesting an audience. So why couldn't Esther have used them?

Presumably things had gone so radically wrong between herself and the king that she was sure any such request would be denied. Furthermore, all official channels were controlled by Haman, and Esther was frightened that he might become suspicious of her.

But did she honestly imagine her husband might have her *killed*? Quite possibly she did. We have already noted the arbitrary nature of absolute power, and that Ahasuerus was not always the most balanced of individuals. A man whose temper was such that he could have the sea whipped for breaking down his bridge, and have the heads of his best engineers lopped off, was liable to do anything! Who *knows* what his advisors might have suggested to him if his second wife had shown herself to be as impertinent as his first? Besides, Esther would have reasoned, what could she hope to achieve even if she did escape with her life? She knew as well as anyone else that Persian law was irrevocable. If an edict had been passed which sentenced the Jews to death, then to death they would inevitably go. What could *anyone* do to save them?

And she must have said to herself , 'Why *should* I stick my neck out in this way? No one need ever know I have anything remotely to do with the Jews. I shall be safe, so long as my true identity isn't discovered. But if people do find out . . .'

Then again, perhaps she thought, 'I've been living a life of decadent Persian luxury in this palace for so many years now, and I've been so thoroughly selfish and materialistic for such a long time, that God wouldn't *want* to use me. I'm unworthy. He uses holy people, not people who haven't wanted anything to do with him.'

As Christians we should know better of course; we who have read the New Testament ought to know that it's never too late to beg God's forgiveness and start again. Simon Peter denied Jesus three times, yet afterwards was used more powerfully than any other apostle except Paul. But it's amazing how often we make the same mistake ourselves, wallowing in our own unworthiness. This kind of false modesty isn't a virtue. It's tantamount to denying God all over again, saying in effect that the sacrifice Jesus made on our behalf is for some reason insufficient. Equally bad is the assumption some church members still make that the only people God really uses are ordained clergymen, while the role of the laity is merely to fill up the pews and cheer their ministers onward.

Having been involved in the leadership of a housechurch, I was astonished to find the same attitudes persisting even there in certain quarters. If you're ill in hospital, no matter if dozens of church members have been to see you, you haven't *really* been visited unless the leader has put in an appearance. There is really no room for this sort of attitude in a church that wants to make an impact on the world around it. The New Testament speaks of the priesthood of all believers (1 Peter 2:5, 9); the task of the leader is to 'equip the saints for the work of ministry' (Ephesians 4:12), not to try to do all the ministry himself. We are *all* God's servants and must live in the expectation of his using us to the full, whether or not we feel worthy to be his instruments.

Esther knew perfectly well that there was no point in

waiting for some priest or rabbi to turn up and rescue the Jews from their plight. She alone was in a position to intervene on their behalf. All in all she must have felt like someone struggling to awake from a nightmare. It wasn't only the fact that she was Jewish. It was that she'd been deceiving her husband all along. As a Zoroastrian, Ahasuerus believed deception to be one of the deadliest sins. To discover simultaneously that his wife was a Semite, a member of the sect outlawed by his First Minister and Favourite, and also a Follower of the Lie was enough to give him apoplexy.

Esther is by no means the only person ever to have been in this sort of predicament, of course. As Christians there are situations in which we have to decide between living a comfortable lie or blowing our cover and admitting to being followers of Jesus. Christian children and teenagers face this kind of dilemma more frequently and more acutely than most adults. Being known as a Christian at school among hostile peers can be exceedingly tough. But at least in Britain it's unlikely to be a matter of life and death. In Saudi Arabia it would be a different matter.

It must have seemed to Esther, as it does to those reading her story, as though the fate of the Jewish race depended entirely upon how she chose to exercise her own free will. We might think that this is a very precarious way for God to work. Yet he will never *force* us to do what he is asking of us. There is always a choice.

Esther makes hers. She sends a message back to her cousin saying she can do nothing. At any rate, this is what I think she says. According to Esther 4:11 her actual words are:

> All the king's officials and people of the royal provinces know that for any man or woman who approaches the king in the inner court without being summoned the king has but one law: that he be put to death. The only exception to this is for the king

to extend the gold sceptre to him and spare his life. But thirty days have passed since I was called to go to the king.

Some readers have argued that this doesn't really mean 'No'. It's more of a cry for help: 'Just look what you're asking me to do.' But I believe that this interpretation springs from a failure to recognize just how far Esther had fallen, how far she had strayed away from her Jewish roots, and, more significantly, from the God who was wanting to use her to save his people.

And it certainly isn't the interpretation that Mordecai puts upon her response. He thinks, as I do, that 'No' is what she means, because instead of offering her sympathy and gentle encouragement, he gets angry. Very angry.

This is not to say that he abandons hope. Quite the reverse. But he sends back a response of his own, so strongly worded that it cannot be summarily dismissed. The battle of wills is now between Mordecai and Esther herself. No longer can she continue to live passively, waiting for things to happen to her, and never making them happen herself. She has reached the turning point of her life.

The content of Mordecai's response is very interesting in itself. First of all he says: 'Do not think that because you are in the king's house you alone of all the Jews will escape' (4:13), implying with these words that Esther's identity will be discovered, regardless of whether she does anything to help her people. He doesn't say how this will come about. Is he threatening to expose her himself if she doesn't tell Ahasuerus the truth about her origins?

Then he says that if she fails to act, 'relief and deliverance for the Jews will arise from another place' (Esther 4:14), a statement with far more significant implications. Mordecai cannot mean anything other than that God will ensure the survival of his people whether Esther decides to work with him or not.

If this is what he means, why doesn't the text make it explicit? Why does the author go to such extraordinary lengths to avoid specifically mentioning God? I believe that he wants us to put two and two together for ourselves. He wants us to look at the way things happen in the world and conclude that there *must* be a God, and one who actively intervenes in the lives of his people. Mordecai clearly believes that God is in ultimate control.

So, if Mordecai had experienced doubt and bitterness against God when the edict had first been issued, he had now put such negative feelings behind him and emerged as a man of quite prodigious faith. So far as he was able to see, the situation had not improved. In fact it had got worse. His people were still condemned to death, and his one hope of saving them – through Esther – had been dashed. Yet he remained confident.

There's an example here for all of us, for faith should not be based on situations as we *see* them at all, but rather upon God. Whatever our circumstances, God has not changed one iota, and not until we've been in straits more dire than Mordecai's have we any excuse for saying otherwise, or for turning our backs on the one who alone can save us. As it says in Psalm 9: 'Those who know you, O Lord, will trust you; you do not abandon anyone who comes to you' (v.10, GNB). But notice the prerequisite. We cannot trust *anyone* unless we know them – God especially, since we cannot see him. How well do we know God? Unless we spend quality time communing with him, the answer has to be 'not very well'. And if this is the case, how will we trust him when the going gets tough?

But was Mordecai right to trust that God must want to save his people? Might his faith not have been misplaced? Why didn't salvation 'arise from another place' for the Jews caught up in the holocaust? Was there someone who could have nipped Hitler's power in the bud in the 1930s, and whom God was calling to do so, but who let him down? Were there others who also let him down, one after another? Why was the holocaust permitted?

Of course, herein lies one of the most vexing theological questions of all time, and one over which Jewish scholars have agonized ever since. Yes, a remnant was preserved, the Jews were saved from total extinction, but 6 million lost their lives, and we are taught that God cares for human beings as individuals, not just as a species. By rejecting Christ as their Messiah, have the Jews placed themselves outside God's protection? Does God always deliver his people from death? The experience of many martyrs would suggest not! All we can say is this: we should not assume that if we neglect the responsibilities God gives us, it won't matter because he'll entrust them to someone else anyway. Haven't you ever thought that the millions of souls on the road to hell represent a holocaust more terrifying than any of the genocides of the twentieth century? And what are we doing about that? The prophet Ezekiel was warned that if he did not speak out to dissuade the wicked man from his ways, 'that wicked man will die for his sin, and I will hold you accountable for his blood' (Ezekiel 33:8). Quite a challenge, is it not? And one thing is certain: if we do reject God's calling, we ourselves will not share in the blessings he wanted to give us. This is exactly the point that Mordecai is about to make to Esther.

For Mordecai goes on to say that Esther herself will die and her father's family will come to an end (Esther 4:14) unless she rises to the challenge facing her. In other words, by ignoring God's will for her life, Esther will be placing herself outside the orbit of God's protection and making herself responsible for the ignominious end of Saul's line.

(As we have already noted, it seems that Esther was the last of the Saulides.)

Finally Mordecai makes the most crucial point in his argument, from which the subtitle of this study of ours has come: 'And who knows but that you have come to royal position *for such a time as this*?' (Esther 4:14).

This statement too carries tremendous implications: that God has been shaping and controlling Esther's circumstances all along in order to bring her to this crucial moment of decision in which she can either find her true destiny or throw it away. The choice is hers. What profound truth there is here! God does shape our lives, but he never imposes his will upon us. We can choose to walk away, or walk his way. If we do walk his way, we are far more likely to find ourselves in the right place at the right time, ready for him to use.

Of course, it is entirely up to God to use us as sparingly or as frequently as he wishes; we hear of no other occasion except this one when he chose to use Esther. Our part is merely to be available. I'm reminded of the comment made by a friend of mine when the person leading the Bible study we were attending drew our attention to the role played by the angel Gabriel in the book of Daniel and at the time of Christ's nativity. Hearing Gabriel described as a 'very busy angel', my friend said: 'Two jobs in five hundred years? I don't call *that* busy!'

But God is much more likely to use us regularly if we stay close to him, spending quality time with him on a daily basis. It has taken me 20 years to accept the truth of this. I used to think it was legalistic to insist on a daily 'quiet time', and that it was OK to dispense with it so long as you were careful to 'practise the presence of God' (to quote Brother Lawrence out of context) – by which I meant gabbling a prayer in the car on the way to the supermarket or whatever. Of course, you can pray anywhere, and at any time, and the more you pray, the better. But if you only pray in two-minute bursts snatched here and there, then don't kid yourself that you're going to become a deeply spiritual person. There are no short cuts to developing a deep relationship with God – or with anyone else, for that matter. If there's no room in your daily schedule for prayer, then change your schedule. Work part time. Hire a cleaner if you can afford one. Get a baby-sitter. Cancel some business appointments. Despite advances in technology and the proliferation of labour-saving devices in our lives, more people in the West are working longer hours than ever before, at the expense of their relationships with families and friends, and to the detriment of their mental and spiritual health.

You may think this sounds rather harsh. You may be saying to yourself, 'It's all very well for *you* to say that we should all change our schedules. But you don't know my circumstances. You don't have my responsibilities.' Or, 'You don't have my childcare commitments.' Or, 'You don't have the money problems I've got.' But the truth is, in our complicated modern lives, we can't afford *not* to pray. The greater our needs, the more we need God to respond to them. There really is no priority more pressing than nurturing your relationship with God. Busyness is the curse of our age. How Satan must laugh when he has us scurrying about like ants, to no good end.

And when you *do* meet with God, and he speaks to you – as he will – write down what he says. I used to believe he never spoke to me at all, until I began to write down the points that occurred to me when I read the Bible or sat in quietness before the Lord. Now I keep three little journals: one to make notes on what I read, one to catalogue my prayers and the answers I receive, and one to record things

I believe God has said to me specifically. It has revolutionized my Christian life.

So, what then is Esther to do? Will she remain silent, abandoning the Jews to their fate and herself to hers? Or will she rise above fate and find her destiny? We realize that ultimately this is a battle of wills not solely between Esther and her cousin, but between Esther and God himself.

9

. . . And a Radical Conversion

Esther sat with Mordecai's letter unrolled upon her lap, and wept.

She didn't understand why she was weeping. She didn't know if she was miserable or angry, in despair or beside herself with indignation. She wanted to tear her cousin's scroll into little pieces and hurl them out of the window like chaff. Yet at the same time, inexplicably, she wanted him to be standing there before her so that she could throw herself into his arms and beg his forgiveness for everything.

'My lady?' the chief of her handmaids ventured. 'My lady, who is the letter from? Why are you so upset? Is there anything I can do?'

'There's nothing you can do. There's nothing anyone can do!' Esther retorted, sweeping the letter to the floor. 'Get out of here and leave me alone!'

Terrified, the poor girl did as she was bidden, leaving her mistress to face her crisis in private. But Esther didn't want to face it. She didn't want to face up to anything, any more than she wanted to face the folk among whom she lived. She wanted to burn the letter and convince herself that it had never existed. She wanted to pretend that the sordid, violent world outside her chambers had never existed either.

Yet in her heart of hearts she knew that none of this was

possible. There was a voice in her head telling her so, a voice she had struggled to ignore ever since coming to the palace. It was quiet but insistent, and somehow seemed to speak with Mordecai's accent. But she was well aware of whose voice it really was, and of what the outcome of her crisis was going to be.

It was to be nothing short of her conversion.

*   *   *

This may strike you as rather an odd word to use in an Old Testament context, especially of someone born a Jew. But it's certainly the right word given the circumstances. Up until this point in her story, Esther has been living solely for herself; now at last she must acknowledge that there is a higher calling upon her life. In a nutshell, she has to recognize God's call and respond to it, though this is not the way in which the author of 'Esther' chooses to express himself. Yet he shows us quite clearly his troubled heroine doing all her growing up at once, and accepting at last who she really is. She can no longer live a lie, pretending to be as Persian, as Aryan, as anyone else at court. In short, she has to repent.

The extra-biblical sections of 'Esther' added to the early Greek version of the book in the Septuagint totally miss the drama of this moment. The Greek adaptor tries very hard – too hard – to be dramatic elsewhere. But the dramatic potential of this particular scene is completely wasted, because he insists on portraying Esther as a paragon of virtue right from page one, pious and resolute, consistently scorning the extravagance of the Persian court.

In the canonical Hebrew version, on the other hand,

Esther 4:15, exactly halfway through the book, forms its pivotal point, upon which all the rest of the story hangs. We have reached the climax to which events have been leading; it is subtly understated rather than laboured in any way. It simply says, 'Then Esther sent this reply to Mordecai.' But from now on, everything is going to be very different.

I'm sure that in the moment of her conversion, Esther felt acutely ashamed – as does every person who truly repents. What a poor witness she had been to Ahasuerus who, whatever his faults, was at least sincere in his devotion to his god. She, on the other hand, had denied hers in everything she had said and done, and even more in the things she hadn't said or done. And she had been perfectly prepared to stand by and see her people annihilated – so long as she survived. I'm reminded of the words of the German theologian Martin Niemoller:

> When Hitler attacked the Jews, I was not a Jew, therefore I was not concerned. When Hitler attacked the Catholics, I was not a Catholic, therefore I was not concerned. When he atacked the unions and the industrialists, I was not a member of a union, therefore I was unconcerned. Then, Hitler attacked *me* – and there was no one left to be concerned.[1]

Perhaps, too, in that moment of enlightenment, Esther suddenly saw the Persian court through God's eyes instead of her own. Her ivory tower was in fact no safe haven of luxury in a brutal world, but a cesspit of immorality into which innocent young girls were taken and debauched, where boys were emasculated, where a mockery was made of God's institution of marriage in which one man and one woman should be united in partnership for life. When

---

1. Martin Niemoller, *Congressional Record* (October 1968).

human beings seek to shake off the shackles of godly morality in this way, they imagine that they are becoming free, whereas in fact they become the slaves of their basest instincts. This is the startling message of the first chapter of Romans. Only in God is true freedom to be found. The courtiers by whom Esther was surrounded were like birds in gilded cages, or rather, they were like the caged wild animals which were from time to time let loose into the king's paradise gardens only in order to be shot in staged hunts.

Soberly counting the cost, Esther now knows that she must risk all in order to save her people. She must risk even death, by appearing before the king unannounced. But paradoxically this puts her in a very powerful position. Having relinquished her very life to God, she has nothing left to lose, and those with nothing to lose are in a sense unassailable.

The truth of this seemingly paradoxical statement has been discovered time and again by dissidents suffering under oppressive regimes. The books of Solzhenitsyn bear particularly clear witness to it. So long as a prisoner has a home, a wife and children, the authorities are able to wield considerable power over him. Once these have all been eliminated, he is much less afraid to take his stand, particularly if he no longer cares whether he himself lives or dies. This is precisely the reason why the Apostle Paul advises us that in times of persecution it is better to remain unmarried (1 Corinthians 7:29–31).

All this enables us more fully to understand Jesus' maxim, 'He who loses his life will find it', for if Esther had tried to cling on to the old life she had, it would undoubtedly have been taken from her. We know that Esther realized all this for herself because she says, 'If I perish, I perish' (Esther 4:16). This is not fatalism; it is total surrender to God.

It also helps us understand something of what that other, most famous, German theologian, Dietrich Bonhoeffer, meant when he wrote in one of his letters from a Nazi prison:

We are left with the only narrow way, a way often hardly to be found, of living every day as if it were our last, yet in faith and responsibility living as though a great future still lay before us. 'Houses and fields and vineyards shall again be bought in this land,' cries the prophet Jeremiah just as the Holy City is about to be destroyed, a striking contrast to his previous prophecies of woe. It is a divine pledge of better things to come, just when all seems blackest. Thinking and acting for the sake of the coming generation, but taking each day as it comes, without fear and anxiety – that is the spirit in which we are being forced to live in practice. It is not easy to be brave and hold out, but it is imperative.'[1]

This exactly describes Esther's situation. Just when things looked blackest for herself and her people, when there was a very grave likelihood that none of them would survive, she had to offer them hope.

The spiritual nature of Esther's conversion is evident from the instructions she proceeds to give to her cousin. She tells him to gather the Jews in Shushan together and fast for three days. The Good News Bible says 'fast and pray'. The Hebrew doesn't say this, but it is certainly implied, because fasting in the Jewish tradition always went hand in hand with prayer; again, the author deliberately avoids using religious language. Esther's message to Mordecai is, in effect, a confession of faith.

The point of fasting was to prepare oneself for com-

1. Dietrich Bonhoeffer, *Letters and Papers from Prison* (SCM Press, 1953).

munion with God and thus to render one's prayers more effective. Fasting is mentioned much more frequently in the post-exilic books of the Old Testament than in those written before the fall of Jerusalem. It is as though the shock of the destruction of the Holy City had added a sense of urgency to the way in which communion with God was regarded.

By asking the Jewish community to fast too, Esther was acknowledging that she needed the support and fellowship of others, and that she was dependent on something more than just human courage.

A three-day fast with no remission at sunset was unusually harsh. Jewish fasts normally lasted for one day only. But these were unusual circumstances. The harshness of the fast reflects the enormity of the crisis. Esther desperately needed to know what God wanted her to do about it. If we are sincere about wanting God's guidance, perhaps this is how serious we have to get.

How to receive and interpret God's guidance is a pressing question in the minds of many Christians. I think most of us can trot out the basic principles. (Listen to your spiritual instincts and to your friends' advice by all means, but measure up any hunches you have against the yardstick of Scripture, etc.) However, we would be wise to remember that guidance is closely connected to obedience. We can't expect God to guide us any further if we haven't obeyed what he's already told us to do. Psalm 25:12 (GNB) says: 'Those who obey the Lord will learn from him the path they should follow.'

Esther had to intercede for the literal survival of her people; we have to intercede for the eternal survival of our non-Christian friends. True intercession is costly. Every great revival throughout the history of the church has been characterized by prayer – hours and hours of prayer, meetings for prayer lasting long into the night over a period of many months or even years. Do we *really* want revival?

However, I should imagine that the Jews responded to her request only too willingly. For by instituting this fast, Esther raised their hopes that, in Bonhoeffer's words, they might have a great future lying before them. Or, indeed, any kind of future. I don't suppose that they minded just then how great it was going to be!

And at once we see that Esther is no longer the passive tool of those around her. Herein lies another profound paradox: now that she has handed over the reins of her life to God, she is in control at last! In finding God, she has found herself, and the confidence to be this person. Perhaps she had felt free when first she had left the restrictive environment of Mordecai's household, and felt powerful when she was crowned queen of the mighty Persian empire, but *now* she has found true liberation, and truly become empowered. Most of us will never be earthly kings or queens or wield significant political power. But as Christians we are brothers and sisters of the King of kings, and have access to *his* power, if only we get to know him well enough to be entrusted with it.

Not only has Esther found God and found herself. Notice that she has begun to act with authority and to lead others – something which we see her doing more and more as the rest of the book unfolds. Esther is now very definitely telling Mordecai what to do, instead of the other way round, for verse 17 says: 'So Mordecai went away and carried out all of Esther's instructions.'

The question of how much authority a woman should wield in the community of God's people, and in particular whether women should ever be given charge over men, has occasioned heated debates and caused grave schisms within the Christian church and also among Jewish synagogues. Reform Judaism allows women to be rabbis; Orthodox

Jewish rabbis are all men. The Roman Catholic Church has no female priests; the Anglican Communion is still sorely divided on the issue. Even among the 'free' churches there is considerable disagreement about whether women should preach or be elders of congregations; whether single women should be cell group leaders, and so on.

Most of the disagreements among Christians have arisen because of the differing emphases placed upon various passages of Scripture – most of which were written by the same person (Paul)! Galatians 3:26–28 says: 'You are all sons of God through faith in Christ Jesus . . . there is neither Jew nor Greek, slave nor free, male nor female.' Whereas 1 Timothy 2:12 says: 'I do not permit a woman to teach or have authority over a man; she must be silent.'

I don't suppose there's much point in my trying to solve in a couple of paragraphs a problem that has plagued the church for generations. But I would just like to put the cat among the pigeons by saying that it is profoundly unhelpful when translators of the Bible camouflage by their choice of language the amount of authority individual women actually held in the churches which Paul founded or with which he had dealings. For example, in Romans 16:1 we meet Phoebe, who in most translations is described as a 'servant', or at best a 'deaconess', in the church at Cenchreae; someone who had been 'a great help to many people'. In fact in the Greek she is descibed as a 'deacon' (the word is used in its masculine form) and she was no 'helper', but a *prostatis*, literally 'she who stands in front' or 'has author-ity'; the word is a noun derived from the verb *proistemi* which in every other occurrence in the New Testament is taken to mean 'to appoint with authority; to preside, govern, superintend'.

I do think that when men start throwing their weight about on the question of masculine authority, it's sometimes a symptom of insecurity. Deep down they are party to the same fear shared by many men outside the church: that in fact the male sex has had its day; there is no room in today's hi-tech world for the hunter/warrior with his excess of testosterone, and once science has perfected cloning, men will be phased out altogether!

But surely there has to be much more to being a man than superior physical strength and blinkered chauvinism? Men who roundly condemn the liberation of women can be as pathetic as Ahasuerus' advisors who feared that society would degenerate into chaos as a result of Vashti refusing to obey her husband's order.

As a matter of fact, I do think that as a rule men *are* more suited by temperament to wielding authority than women are. Although there are obviously exceptions which prove the rule, women by and large are more conscientious than men and therefore liable to take criticism very personally, and to get bogged down in details rather than maintaining the overall vision which an inspiring leader requires. Each of the sexes has its strengths and its weaknesses, and this is as it should be. As in marriage, so in the church and in society as a whole, God made us to complement one another, not to be exactly the same. Also, provided that our leaders lead by inspiring us rather than bludgeoning us with big sticks, most folk of either sex are only too happy to follow. Taking the lead is hard work, as Esther is about to discover.

Returning to the matter of the fast, Esther also promises Mordecai that her slavegirls will fast too. So she now has to admit quite openly to them who she really is.

What a lot of desperate praying must have gone on among Shushan's Jewish population over that three-day period! Have you ever prayed with real desperation for any-thing? As I mentioned before, sometimes it seems as if it's only when we're totally desperate that our prayers begin to have an effect. Sometimes we have to reach rock bottom before God lifts us up. I've often wondered why it is that God lets things go so far and allows us to get into this sort of state before he appears to act.

I think Genesis 32:22–32 holds a key. It's all to do with 'grappling with God'. Here we read the very weird story of Jacob wrestling with God in the shape of an angel until God blesses him. As a result his name was changed from Jacob (meaning 'Twister') to Israel (meaning 'He who grapples with God'). Of course, Israel became the name by which all God's people were known. This implies that the very essence of belonging to God and having a relationship with him involves this grappling. Jacob clung on and kept wrestling and wouldn't let go, even when he got hurt. God wants *us* to be like this, because he wants us to acquire the strength of character he has got. God wants us to grow more like him in every respect. We are his handiwork; as we have already observed, what we become is much more important to him than what becomes of us! This is what being the true Israel is all about: being the people who struggle and who overcome.

This is the secret of real success. Before her conversion, Esther could hardly have been more successful in worldly terms, being married to one of the richest and most power-ful men who had ever lived. But her status had been gained at the expense of her own identity – she couldn't even call herself by the name her parents had given her – and her marriage was on the rocks. To put it in Paul's terms, she had been well and truly 'conformed to this world', whereas after her conversion she is 'transformed by the renewing of her mind'. Indeed, she acquires a mind of her own for the first time!

A very telling example of how we view success was given by Arnold Bell in his talk at Stoneleigh '98 on handling money with faith. He asked members of his audience to imagine that they had just bumped into a couple at the Bible week whom they hadn't seen for ten years, and that they had enquired after the couple's son.

'Oh, he's doing really well,' the couple reply. 'His career has really taken off; he's got a lovely house, and a BMW, and his wife has just given birth to their second child.'

'Very nice,' you say. 'And which church is he involved in these days?'

'Ah.' Their faces fall. 'Well actually, his wife isn't too keen on church, you know, and, well . . .'

So, when asked how their son was doing, these parents ought to have said: 'His life is a disaster! He's completely lost touch with God!' Because *this* is the only success that *really* counts: building a fruitful relationship with God.

This backslidden son had in fact inherited his values from his parents: i.e. their true values as he had perceived them over the years while he was growing up, not the veneer of Christian values they would have professed to be important. Material success and social status were their actual goals, not learning to walk in fellowship with their Creator.

So, going back to Esther, the moment finally comes when she must take her life in her hands and stand before her estranged husband, the king. Will he raise his sceptre to her, or won't he? Again we're on the edges of our seats in suspense. . . .

10

A Banquet and a Seduction

On the third day Esther set aside the sombre garments she had worn while praying, and arrayed herself in all her splendour. When she was dressed in her royal robes, she called upon the omniscient God her preserver, then took two maids along with her. Upon one she leaned for support, while the other followed, carrying her train. Esther was blushing and in the bloom of her beauty, her face was as cheerful as it was lovely, but her heart was in the grip of fear.

She passed through all the doors and entered the royal presence. The king was seated on his throne in the fullness of his majesty. He was all gold and precious stones, a breathtaking spectacle. He looked up, his face radiant with regal dignity, and glared at his wife in a towering rage. The queen fell, changing colour in a faint, and swooning on the shoulder of the maid who went before her.

Then God changed the spirit of the king to gentleness, and in deep concern he leapt from his throne and took her in his arms until she came to herself. He soothed her with reassuring words: 'Esther, what is it? Don't be afraid of me, your loving husband. You shall not die, for our edict is only for our subjects. Come to me.' And the king lifted his golden sceptre and laid it upon her neck. Then he kissed her and said: 'You may address me.'

She answered, 'Oh my lord, I saw you looking like an angel of God, and I was awestruck at your glorious appearance. Your countenance is so full of grace, my lord, that I look on you in wonder.' But even while she was speaking, she collapsed again in a faint. The king was distressed, and all his attendants comforted her.

*   *   *

Whew! Well what did you reckon to *that* purple passage of narrative? Over the top, or what? Did you think for a moment that I must have got carried away upon a wave of sentimental Victorian self-indulgence? All that blushing and swooning and fainting . . . it's like the action from a silent film. We can readily imagine the scene being played out on the silver screen complete with sepia tones, jerky frames and piano accompaniment, and visualize the dialogue being flashed up on cards before our eyes.

Just don't blame me, that's all. Because the description is lifted – or rather, translated verbatim – straight from the Greek text of 'Esther' as found in the Apocrypha ('The Rest of the Chapters of the Book of Esther' 15:1–16). And it demonstrates perfectly the Greek adaptor's predilection for mawkish melodrama at the expense of the genuinely powerful but admittedly laconic drama of the Hebrew original. He ruins everything, not solely with all the swooning, but by having the king refer explicitly to the edict against the Jews, when in fact at this stage in proceedings he would have no reason whatever to associate it with his wife. When Esther appeared before him unannounced in the throne room that day, Ahasuerus can't have had any inkling at all as to what had prompted her to embark upon such a drastic course of action. In fact we know this to be the case, from the way the story later unfolds. But by the time the Greek adaptor set about his literary task, the genre of the Greek novel had well and truly emerged, in which gushing romanticism was *de rigueur*.

To my mind the scene in its original Hebrew version is perfect just as it is: unembellished, understated, and all the more effective as a result. There's no blushing or fainting, no excuse for the king to sweep Esther into his arms in a Mills and Boon embrace. All it tells us is that on the third day of her fast, Esther put on her royal robes and went before the king: 'When he saw her, he was pleased with her and held out to her the gold sceptre' (Esther 5:2). There is no reference at all to the edict against the Jews. In that moment it could hardly have been further from Ahasuerus' mind.

Understated and unembellished as this simple account may be, clearly there was nothing understated or unembellished about Esther's appearance. Both Hebrew writer and Greek adaptor are at pains to tell us that their heroine is no longer dressed for mourning, even though she has not broken her fast. She has got herself dolled up in her finest and is made up to the nines. Whatever the reason for her having been out of favour, she now banks on the fact that the king must be missing her in the same way he'd missed Vashti. When he sees her she wants him to remember exactly what he's been missing. . . .

In other words, in contrast to Vashti, who refused to exploit her own sexuality when Ahasuerus demanded it of her, Esther was prepared to play hers for all it was worth. How are we to square this with our claim that she has been 'converted'? In fact, there is no actual incompatibility here. Esther was using her charms upon her own husband, after all.

And there is nothing 'dualist' about Judaism, any more

than there should be about Christianity. The contrast drawn frequently by Paul and others between 'flesh' (bad) and 'spirit' (good) is not a contrast between the physical and the invisible, but between living according to unregenerate human nature and living in fellowship with God. The Judaeo-Christian belief, which is strikingly holistic in nature, is that God created the body as well as the soul, the material world just as surely as the spiritual, and there is nothing inferior or illusory about it. There are no souls-without-bodies in the Bible; even in heaven we shall have 'spiritual bodies' (admittedly a mind-boggling concept). Much Greek philosophy *was* dualist, teaching that the soul as a spiritual entity is trapped inside the body and longs for freedom from it. (This kind of thinking was probably influenced in turn by Indian ideas, and became popular in Greece in reaction against the way that many Greeks idolized youth and beauty.) The suspicion that sex is somehow dirty or unworthy of a spiritual person ought to have no place in Christian doctrine. The Song of Songs is an entire book devoted to the celebration of physical love within marriage.

By now you should be able to see what I mean when I say that Esther isn't exactly a champion of feminism! True, she's no discredit to womanhood, emerging ultimately as 'a canny political actor who manages to rule a king – a far cry from those homey Mothers of Israel who want only sons' (Rachel Brownstein in *Out of the Garden* again). But many modern feminists baulk at the suggestion that a woman should have to use her sexuality in order to become empowered.

Yet in Esther's day what other means did women have at their disposal? Politically they were utterly disenfranchised. We can only guess whether Esther would have used the same or different methods if her story had been set in our century instead of hers.

What scene would have greeted Esther as she stood there before her exalted husband? The throne room, known as the Apadana ('hall of pillars'), must have been an intimidating place. If it was anything like the one at Persepolis – and it is very likely to have been identical – it was huge, and enormously high, with six rows of six soaring fluted columns crowned by elegant carvings of bulls or gryphons set back to back. You approached this hall by means of a grand stairway, and entered through massive cedar-wood doors plated with brass. At the far end was a dais, and here sat the king, on a high-backed golden chair with silver lion's feet; the legs and feet of his footstool were in the form of bull's legs and hooves. In his right hand he held his sceptre, which was long and slender with a jewelled knob on the end. Two smoking incense burners were positioned in front of the dais, and over the top of it there was a tasselled canopy inlaid with jewels and supported by golden poles. The canopy was decorated with rosettes and also adorned by the symbol of Ahura-Mazda, the winged disc of the sun, saluted by roaring lions. Behind the king his page boys and advisors would have been standing. Esther must have taken a very deep breath before proceeding any further.

But her gamble was about to succeed beyond her wildest dreams. As soon as she walks, uninvited, into the audience chamber, Ahasuerus not only extends to her the golden sceptre – which means that her life is spared – but he calls her 'Queen', thus affirming that her royal status is unimpaired. Notice the striking contrast here between the long drawn-out fast, and the speed with which the prayers prayed during the course of it are answered. When something is totally saturated in prayer, this is precisely the kind of result which can and does ensue.

The king also promises Esther that, whatever her request,

he will grant it, 'even up to half the kingdom'(5:3). The use of this phrase probably owes nothing to fairy tale and everything to actual practice. It is likely that it was a stock phrase, a formula used by Middle Eastern kings, and the reason why it appears here, just as it appears in tales of the kind we read in *The Arabian Nights*, is because it is exactly what Ahasuerus would have said. The use of the formula indicated that you were highly favoured; but just as a king was expected to use it, so *you* were expected not to hold him to his promise! This would hardly be very polite, and instead of being given anything at all, you would probably wind up losing your head.

Incidentally, the same phrase is also used by King Herod after Salome has danced her 'dance of the seven veils' (see Mark 6:23). It is interesting to compare the two situations: both involve women using their sexual wiles upon kings, and both of these women elicit the same response – but what each of them proceeds to ask for could hardly be more different. Salome wants the death of John the Baptist; Esther wants life for her people.

But she doesn't fall at her husband's feet and plead for her people straight away, as we might expect her to. The suspense is kept up, because she merely invites Ahasuerus and Haman to be her guests at supper.

Why? Well, there are a number of possible reasons, and Esther had probably thought of most of them. First and foremost, she knew that it would be unwise to make any political request of Ahasuerus when he was sitting there surrounded by his advisors. She wanted to get him in private, where their influence would not be so immediate.

It was an exceedingly unusual thing to do, though. As we said earlier, king and queen might dine together, but only in private. If guests were involved, the sexes were generally segregated. Haman would have been shocked but deeply honoured to be included in the queen's invitation.

So, no longer is Haman to be the manipulator. From this point on, it is Esther who does the manipulating. Whereas Vashti fell from grace as a result of her refusal to be the king's guest, Esther would win back her place in his heart by being his hostess.

Notice that when Esther invites the king and his minister to dine with her, the banquet has already been prepared (Esther 5:4). She has truly acted in faith; she is convinced that God has guided her into issuing her invitation, so she has already begun to prepare for its being accepted.

This is the exact opposite of the concept of 'tempting fate', the idea that, for example, it's bad luck to decorate a baby's bedroom before it is born in case 'something goes wrong'. There is no room for this kind of superstition in the life of a Christian. Sometimes we just have to move ahead in faith, as the priests of Moses' successor Joshua had to do when they led God's people across the Jordan and back into the Promised Land. When Moses had parted the Red Sea (Exodus 14:21–22) it had already become dry land by the time the Israelites started to cross. But on the second occasion (Joshua 3), it was not until the priests actually stepped into the river that its waters began to recede, for God was requiring more faith from them this time.

Each of us can probably cite similar examples from our own Christian lives. For instance, when Keith and I were starting our gospel choir, we had no experience or qualifications in the field, and modest ability. We had no idea where we were going to find either enough teenagers with good voices who wanted to use their talents for God in this way, or venues in which to perform. But we strongly believed that God was telling us to go ahead. So we made preparations accordingly, and God has blessed us all along the way.

So the king and Haman accept Esther's invitation. That evening they go together to the queen's apartment to dine. And what an emotionally charged occasion this must have been. . . .

*   *   *

On one couch sat Haman the Amalekite, who was striving very hard to refrain from grinning like a monkey. For here he was, reclining at table with the King and Queen of Persia! No one outside of the royal family itself had ever been accorded such an honour. What a truly remarkable man he must be! And never in his life had he dined so superbly. State banquets were one thing, but this was something else! Everything was dainty and perfect, in proportion to the intimate scale of the party. The tiniest creatures and birds had been deftly gutted and stuffed, and garnished with the most mouthwatering of sauces. There were snails cooked in their shells, and the sweetest baby vegetables all exquisitely dressed and served. For dessert there were lemons which had been hollowed out and filled with sherbet, and bite-sized pastries filled with mincemeat and glazed with honey.

As a man who was unfailingly meticulous in all that he did, Haman was well placed to appreciate evidence of painstaking preparation and close attention to fine detail wherever he came across it. And so enraptured was he by everything he saw, for once in his life he neglected to ask himself what was really going on around him, and what his part in it was supposed to be. He was quite simply so convinced of his superiority to other men that it did not occur to him to question his right to be there.

Ahasuerus, on the other hand, was in uncharacteristically pensive mood. He could not imagine why Esther should have risked her life for the sake of inviting him and his First Minister round for supper. He knew there had to be more to all this than met the eye, yet was frankly afraid to ask Esther outright what it was, in case it was something which ought to be perfectly obvious to anyone but a fool. Besides, he didn't really want to talk to Esther at all. He wanted to carry her straight off to her bedroom and renew his acquaintance with her peerless body rather than play guessing games with her mind. By all the gods, how could he have forgotten how ravishingly beautiful she was?

Meanwhile Esther herself simply smiled becomingly, laughed prettily, and engaged in innocuous small talk. She appeared totally at her ease: relaxed, happy, in command. Indeed she *was* in command, in the sense that the two men were there at her invitation, and it was her prerogative to set the agenda for the evening. But she was far from relaxed, or happy. Although her feelings were carefully hidden from her guests, they were in turmoil. Fear for her people, longing for her husband, hatred for Haman, and in spite of all this, faith that with the help of her God she would yet accomplish what she knew was being asked of her – all these emotions were surfacing in her heart. All that was required of her was patience, and the ability to respond to God's prompting when the right time came.

At length, when the meal was over and the three of them were tarrying over their wine, Ahasuerus could stand the suspense no longer. Unable to believe that Esther did not want *something*, he begged her to tell him what it was, and again promised her up to half of his kingdom.

'All right,' she answered with a smile, her dark eyes dancing above the rim of her wine cup. 'What I should like, my lord, is for you and Haman your friend to come to another supper here tomorrow evening.' And with that the king had to be content.

*   *   *

So, why all this stalling? Was Esther suffering from nerves, and trying to postpone the evil moment for as long as possible? I don't think so. I think she was firmly in control now, both of herself and of the situation. She wanted Ahasuerus so intrigued and so maddened with desire that he would eat out of her hand the way he'd been eating out of Haman's. She was seducing him.

Suddenly it seems singularly appropriate that Esther's name is derived from that of Ishtar, goddess of love. Ishtar was goddess of war, too, but the relevance of this does not emerge until later.

Why did Esther keep inviting Haman as well? The reason why she invited him to the *second* supper will soon become deliciously obvious. But I think she invited him to the first one because she wanted to deprive the king of the opportunity to 'know her' in the biblical sense again too soon. She wanted to excite his desire but not to let him satisfy it, not until she had got what she wanted. Also, I think she wanted Haman to realize, eventually, that when it came to manipulation, he'd now met more than his match. To begin with he doesn't even remotely suspect that Esther has any ulterior motive.

For at the first supper Esther lulls Haman into a false sense of security so serene that by the time he comes to retire, he's walking on air, convinced he is uniquely favoured by his master's glamorous wife. His pride is given time to swell before it bursts.

But at the second banquet she will make him squirm as he's never squirmed before.

11

Haman Eats Humble Pie

The next episode in the story provides a delicious example of God casting down the proud and exalting the meek in their stead. Mordecai, the faithful retainer who once upon a time saved the king's life, is exalted, while the braggart Haman – who has been the king's favourite for much too long and for no good reason – is suitably humiliated before tumbling spectacularly from his pedestal. . . .

*　　　*　　　*

When Haman departed from Esther's first banquet he was euphoric. He had eaten and drunk a great deal, and everything in his rose-tinted world was wonderful. Indeed, the ambitious Amalekite had never felt happier or more pleased with himself in all his selfish and upwardly mobile life, for it appeared at last that his months and years of careful scheming had well and truly paid off. He sensed that he was now completely trusted, not only by the king, but also by the queen, whom Haman had long believed to be by far the more shrewd and intelligent of the two. While Haman had been reasonably satisfied with himself when he had successfully gained Ahasuerus' confidence, he was infinitely more jubilant now that he had won over the queen as well. For if *she* were to whisper the occasional good word about him in the imperial ear, Haman was convinced that his future as the most influential man in the whole of Persia was assured.

How clever he had been to charm this remarkable woman so comprehensively! How delightful it had been to hear her laugh so prettily at his jokes, and to see her smile in open admiration of his witty conversation. She was so beautiful, too, when she smiled. Her teeth were dainty and perfect; when she threw back her head to laugh, her neck was long and white as a swan's. And the way she had glanced at him, every now and again, across the rim of her wine cup . . . Haman even dared to wonder whether one day she might invite him to her apartment for something a little more titillating than a convivial meal.

Then suddenly, unexpectedly, Haman's bubble was burst even before he got home, and the sweet taste that lingered in his mouth turned abruptly sour. For sitting by the palace gate as he walked past was Mordecai the Jew.

Mordecai didn't throw himself down at Haman's feet the way everyone was supposed to. Even now, when his stubborn lack of respect had condemned him and all his people to death, he didn't so much as get up from his seat. He simply studied the king's First Minister with silent, smouldering malevolence, his eyes communicating more eloquently than any words could have done his total and profound contempt.

Haman was furious. What right had such a pathetic creature to despise *him*, Grand Vizier of Persia? What right had this Jew not to be terrified of the man who had sealed his death warrant, along with that of all his verminous people? Wasn't it supposed to be easier to make men fear you than it was to earn their respect? Yet it seemed that in the case of Mordecai, Haman could achieve neither.

Haman was so angry, he could have grasped the lousy little rat by the ears and twisted them around hard enough to give his enemy no choice but to grovel howling in the dust before him.

But at the same time he knew he'd had far too much wine, and that he must not let drink do the talking for him, let alone the acting. He knew full well how boorish and cowardly such violent behaviour would appear to anyone who witnessed it. So somehow he controlled himself, and went on walking home.

Approaching his house, he heard voices and laughter, and saw the welcome glow of lighted lamps in the gaps around the shutters. He could pick out from the cordial hubbub the voice of Zeresh, his faithful wife, and those of some of their closest friends. Beginning to feel rather better, more like himself, he pushed the door open and swaggered inside. Then inviting those present to gather around him, he started to boast of how rich he was, and of how many strapping sons he had. He also bragged about the multifarious ways in which the king had showered him with honours and promoted him above the heads of everyone else at court.

'And that's not all,' he concluded triumphantly, dimly aware that he was slurring his speech. 'I'm the only man whom the queen has ever invited to dine with herself and the king. She's invited me again for tomorrow!'

But he couldn't keep it up. He couldn't forget the defiance on Mordecai's face or his stubbornness in refusing yet again to bow the knee before him. Giving way to drunken tears, Haman slumped head in hands on the table and blurted out his bitterness like a spoilt child. 'None of it means a thing to me! Not so long as I see that Jew sitting by the palace gate every time I walk through it.'

His wife and friends tried to console him by reminding him that Mordecai wouldn't be there for very much longer. Soon enough he and all his kind would be wiped from the face of the earth. But Haman would not be placated. He didn't want to have to walk past his enemy and witness his defiance even one more time.

'Then don't,' his friends suggested. 'Make him an example; get rid of him straight away. We'd be only too happy to help. We'll build you a gallows, right here and now in your own back garden. In the morning you can ask the king to have Mordecai hanged upon it without delay, and then you can go to tomorrow's banquet with a spring in your step and a song in your heart.'

Haman was delighted. He couldn't have thought of a niftier plan himself. Pouring himself yet another glass of wine, he sat and sipped it smugly while his friends staggered to and fro by torchlight with planks of wood and hammers and built the most obscenely enormous gallows anyone had ever seen. Suspended 22 metres from the ground, the dangling Mordecai would be visible from every rooftop in Shushan.

*   *   *

If this episode (found in Esther 5:9–14) were taken from a Greek story rather than from a Jewish one, we might say that at this point in the proceedings Haman was suffering from a serious attack of hubris. Hubris is a concept familiar to students of Greek tragedy; it is defined by the Collins English Dictionary as 'an excess of ambition, pride, etc., ultimately causing the transgressor's ruin'. It is closely linked in Greek with *ate*, madness. The Greeks had a saying,

'Whom the gods would destroy, they first make mad', and we see the process graphically illustrated in many of the best ancient Greek plays. But in a sense this idea exists in every culture; it's summed up in our own proverb, 'pride goes before a fall', which in itself derives from the biblical book of Proverbs. And indeed, there is something about this passage – what with Haman's extravagant boasting and the ridiculous size of the gallows he has built – which leaves the reader in no doubt that he is going to get his come-uppance, and not a moment too soon.

. On the subject of the gallows itself, I understand that in the twentieth century during the Iranian Revolution and the years that followed, the Iranian government used to hang dissidents from builders' cranes by way of public display. It has been common practice in Persia/Iran throughout history to hang convicted criminals as high up as possible, as a warning to others.

What was it about Mordecai's defiance that aggravated Haman so much? The former had nothing, the latter everything – wealth, power, and no shortage of sons to inherit it. (According to Esther 9:13 he had ten, but notice that when he is boasting about them in 5:11, along with all his wealth and privileges, it's the money he calls to mind first!) Yet deep down Haman recognized that those who have nothing have nothing to lose, whereas he himself was vulnerable in the extreme. Inwardly anxious, and subject to violent mood swings, he was not even master of his own emotions. Monarchs, presidents and prime ministers can *seem* supremely powerful. But if they do not have power over themselves they can be brought down very swiftly. (Witness the number of politicians whose careers have been ended through an inability to control their sexual desires.) You cannot hope to govern others if you are unable to govern yourself.

At this point we are treated to one of those wonderful examples of perfect timing which make the book of Esther such a consummate masterpiece. In a passage packed with the most deliciously excruciating irony, while Haman and his cronies are engaged in building their gallows, we the readers are whisked away, and it's 'meanwhile back at the ranch' time. The scene shifts to the palace during the very same night, and we learn that Ahasuerus is plagued by a bout of insomnia. He decides to have an attendant read to him from the royal records.

Why didn't Ahasuerus get out a scroll and read it for himself? The answer may be very simple: it's quite possible that he *couldn't* read. Persia was not a particularly literate society, and reading may have been considered the job of specialized scribes. The king may well have deemed reading beneath him. In the education of a Persian king, learning to ride and to shoot with the bow and the importance of telling the truth were reckoned much more important. Unlike the Babylonians, the Persians were not great intellectuals. Scribes, doctors, mathematicians and the like tended to come from Babylon.

But why the royal records? Maybe they were boring enough to send *anyone* to sleep! Or maybe the king was feeling insecure, as he often did, and wanted to be reminded of his achievements, such as they were. The Talmud suggests that Ahasuerus was sleepless because he was troubled about why Esther had invited Haman to the banquet as well as himself, and suspected that the two of them might be hatching a plot to kill him. He wanted the records read out so that he could see if there was anyone at court who hadn't been properly rewarded for some service rendered to the state and who might therefore have undertaken to poison his security staff against him so that they were covering up for the conspirators.

Anyhow, his attendant begins to read to the king as directed, and presently happens to reach the section about Mordecai discovering an earlier plot on Ahasuerus' life. Ahasuerus interrupts, wanting his memory refreshed as to how Mordecai was rewarded. Someone who performed a great service for the Persian king was customarily accorded the title of Benefactor, and his name was entered on a special list. He might be given a huge grant of land, a whole wardrobe of expensive clothing, horses, gold ornaments or some other lavish material reward. But the king is told that there is no record of Mordecai having been rewarded at all.

Ahasuerus declares that this appalling oversight must be put right straight away, and that the reward must be especially noteworthy, to make amends for nothing having been done already. He wonders what might be appropriate, but true to form cannot reach a decision without consulting his advisors. So he asks who else is up and about, and is told that Haman is hanging around waiting to see him; presumably the Grand Vizier has been reluctant to disturb his master at too early an hour lest he put him in an uncooperative mood. (Haman, by contrast, can't have been to bed all night. Pure adrenaline is keeping him going.)

There is wonderful irony here. It turns out that Haman, to whom 'auspicious times' are so important, couldn't have chosen a worse time to visit the king. Of course, his timing proves to be perfect from the author and the reader's point of view. . . .

Haman is brought in, and the scene begins to read like a reversal of the old children's story about the gardener who lost his shears and heaped curses upon whoever had stolen them – only to find that he'd stuck them behind his own ear. The king asks Haman to suggest how a distinguished benefactor whom he particularly wishes to honour might be rewarded, and Haman, arrogant knave that he is, naturally assumes that Ahasuerus can't be talking about anyone but *him*. So he suggests that the man be dressed in one of the king's own robes and placed upon a horse which the king has ridden, and which has its mane dressed in the way that only the king's horse would have it. Then the man should be led around the city by a highly important minister who must proclaim: 'This is what is done for the man the king delights to honour!' (Esther 6:9).

Haman really is betraying his own empty delusions of grandeur here. Thinking that he himself was about to be handsomely rewarded, he could have asked for the governorship of some huge tract of the empire. But no, he wants to dress up in the king's robes and go riding around on the king's horse. He seems to want to be accorded equality with the king, or even with a god. This seems to be what he's been wanting all along.

'Great idea!' the king must have responded, when Haman had had his say. 'I knew I could rely on you to come up with a brilliant proposal. Go, find my servant Mordecai, and see to it straight away.'

What a marvellous moment this is. It's every bit as cleverly crafted as some of the moments in Sophocles' *Oedipus Rex*, one of the very finest Greek tragedies, in which the audience knows exactly who Oedipus really is and why he is heading for disaster, while he blunders on in ignorance. Of course, Haman himself ends up having to parade his arch-enemy through the streets of Shushan.

But stranger things have happened. As they say, fact can be stranger than fiction, and especially when God muscles in on the act! When I was first going out with Keith, and he'd just become a Christian but I hadn't yet done so, he let me down one day. He'd promised to take me out walking at the weekend, but then forgotten all about it and arranged to go out with a curator from the local musuem to do some geology. I created a big scene and said, 'Fine way for a Christian to behave!' and so on and so forth. Keith said, 'Pray for snow, then. Only snow stops geologists.' So I did, in a belligerent sort of way, and when I woke up on the Saturday morning, the world was white! I always get excited when it snows, and it was quite a few moments before I realized that I had more than one reason for being excited at *this* particular snowfall.

Don't get me wrong. I'm not saying that every single coincidence in our lives has been deliberately brought about by meticulous divine planning. If your favourite colour is red and you meet someone else whose favourite colour is red, this is unlikely to have any profound spiritual meaning – or to be a heavenly sign for making a marriage proposal on the spot! But some coincidences clearly *are* an indication that God is at work in our lives, especially when we add them all together, or when they happen as a result of prayer, or when we look back across the years and see how our lives have been shaped once we have placed them into the hands of our Creator, or even before. The one day we happen to buy a newspaper we don't normally read, and see advertised in it the very job we've been looking for; the one time we miss our train home, only to discover later that it has been involved in an accident . . . the more closely we walk with God, the more coincidences of this nature will happen to us, and the more we will realize that God *is* looking after us, all the time, causing things to 'work together for good' (Romans 8:28) even when we seem unable to hear him speaking to us directly.

Wouldn't you just love to have seen Mordecai and Haman's procession take place? There are some events in history I would really like to have been present to witness, and this is one of them. The citizens must have been agog, especially the Jews, who will have been wondering what it could possibly mean. I'd guess that Haman wanted the ground to swallow him up, but what of Mordecai? Did *he* enjoy the experience? Was he even told why it was happening? Perhaps he suspected that it might be some bizarre religious ritual which was going to end in his death. There *were* religious festivals in the ancient world which involved someone being treated as a king for the day and then ritually killed. These were the kind of festivals we have mentioned already: Saturnalia and the like. Very many Saturnalia customs were about things being turned on their heads, and that's exactly what *this* incident is about.

There is a marvellous little passage in the Talmud which I can't resist quoting here. While I'm not sure that it contributes significantly to our understanding of the story, it certainly adds something! It says:

> As Mordecai was being led down the street where Haman lived, Haman's daughter saw them. She thought that the man on the horse was her father and that the man walking before him was Mordecai. So she took a chamber pot and emptied it on her father's head. When he looked up and she saw who it was, she threw herself from the roof to the ground and killed herself.

Actually this isn't the only contribution that the Talmud has to offer on the subject. Another passage says:

> After Haman had trimmed Mordecai's hair he dressed him and said: 'Mount and ride.' Mordecai replied: 'I can't; I'm weak from fasting.' So Haman had to stoop down, and Mordecai climbed on his back. When Mordecai was up, he gave Haman a kick. Haman said to him, 'Is it not written in your books: Rejoice not when thine enemy faileth?' 'Ah,' Mordecai answered, 'That only applies when your enemy is an Israelite. In regard to *you* folk it is written: And thou shalt tread upon their high places.'

Well! Enough of the Talmud. Time to return to the Bible. It strikes me that the only person involved in this episode upon whom the irony of it all would have been utterly lost, was Ahasuerus himself. The king had never yet been told anything about the enmity between Haman and Mordecai. To begin with, Haman had hoped he never would find out, because he hadn't wanted the king to put two and two together and realize that the people Haman was intending to wipe out were the Jews. Now, when he *did* want to bring his enmity with Mordecai to the king's attention, so that he might get permission to have the rascal hanged, he found himself quite unable to do so. The last thing he wanted was for Ahasuerus to start asking the sort of questions which might lead to his finding out that Haman's enemy and the benefactor who had saved His Imperial Majesty from assassination were one and the same.

So while Haman is parading Mordecai round his capital city, Ahasuerus remains in his ivory tower, blissfully unaware of the astonishment which the spectacle is undoubtedly provoking. Ahasuerus may be the most powerful man in the world on paper, but in practice he's something of a stooge.

Afterwards Haman creeps away home, covering his face in shame. (The phrase 'covering his face' will be used again presently; its initial appearance here is pregnant with foreboding.)

Have you ever been shown up like this? There's a sure way to ensure it never happens – don't put yourself on a pedestal or let anyone else put you on one, then you can't get knocked off. If we are humble and modest, this kind of thing can't happen. We are not supposed to grovel and harp on about our own unworthiness all the time. (I'm reminded of *Monty Python and the Holy Grail* where God looks down from the clouds and shouts, 'Stop grovelling! I detest grovellers!') But if we set ourselves up as paragons rather than recognizing that we are merely redeemed sinners, we ask for trouble.

Another piece of advice on this subject is suggested in Psalm 34: keep your eyes fixed on God, not on yourself. Verse 5 says: 'Those who look to him are radiant; their faces are never covered with shame.'

Afterwards Haman's wife and 'wise friends' (surely the author is being sarcastic here) commiserate with him by saying just about the last thing he would have wanted to hear: 'Since Mordecai . . . is of Jewish origin, you cannot stand against him – you will surely come to ruin' (Esther 6:13). It's as though now that everything is going wrong for Haman, his wife and friends are wanting to distance themselves from him and give the impression that they have had nothing whatever to do with the course of action he's been pursuing. Haman is already becoming isolated, because a man of his character is unlikely to have the sort of friends who will stand by him in a crisis.

The wording seems to imply too that they knew or at least suspected that there was something special and indomitable about the Jewish race; that it occupied a unique place in God's purposes. This prediction of Haman's ultimate downfall also fuels the suspense, as we wait for it to be fulfilled.

I think that while to some Christians huge tracts of the Old Testament are a closed book, others of us are so familiar with much of it that we fail to appreciate how brilliantly constructed it is. Perhaps some of the best stories have been spoiled for us by the fact that we first encountered them as children, when obviously we couldn't grasp how sophisticated they were, and so we were introduced to them in simplified versions in which a great deal was lost. Consequently as adults we make the mistake of thinking that we know all there is to know about them, so we gloss over them much too quickly.

Much of 'Esther', like the Joseph sagas in Genesis, works so well because the author allows us, his readers, to see the whole picture, whereas the characters involved are operating partly in the dark and so can dig themselves enormous pits into which we subsequently watch them fall. Somehow this makes us like God, omniscient. For once, the clouds of human ignorance roll back, and we understand how, in spite of the schemes of men, God's purposes will ultimately prevail. We see this very clearly in 'Esther' without God even needing to be mentioned. Only when we genuinely get to grips with what the biblical text is saying do we fully perceive how much is said with so few words. Truly Scripture *is* inspired!

12

Hoist With His Own Petard

In many ways the next chapter of 'Esther' (chapter 7) forms the climax of the book. We might be forgiven, in fact, for imagining that at the end of this chapter, it's all over bar the shouting. But things aren't quite that simple.

*   *   *

From the moment he arrived at Esther's second supper, Haman felt himself to be at a distinct disadvantage. This was a feeling he didn't like at all, since he'd grown used to being the master of every circumstance in which he found himself, and it made him extremely nervous. Having been up all the previous night contriving Mordecai's downfall, the hapless Grand Vizier had then been forced to spend the entire day toting his sworn enemy the length and breadth of Shushan. He'd made himself hoarse by having to announce to all and sundry that this was how the Great King of Persia chose to honour his most worthy benefactor. As if all these things weren't bad enough, he hadn't had time to get himself properly ready for the second supper, because the king's eunuchs had arrived to escort him to it while he was still pouring out his sorrows to his wife and friends.

So there he was – a man who habitually prided himself on his impeccable grooming – with his hair uncombed and unscented and his clothes noticeably crumpled, trying desperately to disguise the fact that he was all of a fluster. He wished that he could enjoy the honour of being Esther's guest, as he had done on the previous occasion. But the taste of mortification was still bitter in his mouth. Also – and this was something even more disconcerting – he found himself beginning to be suspicious as to whether the business with Mordecai and his own sudden popularity with the queen might not somehow be connected. So as the evening progressed, he sank further and further into depression. But the king didn't notice.

For while Haman slouched brooding over his wine, Ahasuerus' attention was fully taken up with his wife. How stunning she looked tonight; what promise there was in her glittering eyes, what depth, what mystery. He couldn't under-stand how he could have let thirty days go past without summoning her to his bed. How could he possibly have allowed the relationship between them to turn sour? Gazing raptly upon her, he couldn't even remember how things had ever gone wrong. All he wanted to do was to clasp her in his arms and make her his own once more. In fact he very nearly did so, for Haman was being so uncharacteristically morose that Ahasuerus temporarily forgot he was even there.

Noting with quiet satisfaction the desire that smouldered in her husband's eyes, Esther smiled, deliberately fanning it into flame. Instinctively the king moved up closer towards her, but her response was to inch away from him by precisely the same amount.

'My darling, my queen, what is it that you want of me?' Ahasuerus implored her. 'Only tell me, please, and you shall have it, I swear.' And for a third time he offered her up to half of his kingdom.

The time was ripe at last, and Esther knew it. The king was visibly drooling, and more than ready to eat out of her elegantly manicured hand.

'My lord,' she said, lowering her eyes demurely now so that the lengthened lashes swept her cheekbones. 'My lord, if I have found favour with you, and if it pleases Your Majesty, grant me my life, and the lives of my people. For we have been betrayed, my lord. We have been sold – sold for destruction, for slaughter, for annihilation! This is the request I have been wanting to make of you, O noblest one. Perhaps now you see why I was afraid, and shrank from putting it to you earlier.'

But Ahasuerus did not see at all – any more than Esther had imagined that he would do. Nor did he see Haman's fingers tremble around his wine cup while the colour drained from his face like water from a punctured skin. All he saw was his lovely wife sitting so helplessly in front of him, irresistibly lost and vulnerable in a way he had never seen her before, with a single silent tear slipping down her velvet cheek, and he was undone.

However, before he could open his mouth to ask what dreadful fantasy could possibly have taken root in her fertile mind, she had leaned forward urgently towards him and placed her little hands on his wrists. 'My lord,' she continued, 'if we had merely been sold as slaves, I would have kept quiet, for I would not venture to trouble Your Gracious Majesty with trivialities. But we have an enemy who will not rest until every last one of us is dead.' Then she sat back and watched as the king was consumed by anger – precisely as she had hoped and known that he would be. Her plan was working to perfection.

'Who is this enemy?' Ahasuerus demanded. 'Where is the man who would dare to do such a monstrous thing?'

With disarming simplicity Esther spoke his name; but there was scarcely any need for her to do so, for Haman had already dropped his wine cup in terror, and its contents were spreading like blood all over the floor.

*   *   *

What a truly brilliant scene the author of 'Esther' has painted for us here at the beginning of Esther chapter 7. Every line is shot through with irony and suspense; Hitchcock would have been proud to have crafted anything half so delicious! Esther chooses the most highly charged moment imaginable to make of her royal husband the request we've all been waiting for – but oh, how cleverly she introduces it! Without any initial explanation, but aiming for maximum dramatic effect, she asks the king to grant her her life and that of her people, for she and they have been 'sold for destruction'.

This emotive expression is a reference to Haman's offering to enrich the treasury with the Jews' confiscated property. But actually Esther doesn't use only the one noun, 'destruction'. She uses three: 'destruction, slaughter and annihilation' (Esther 7:4). She is deliberately echoing the terminology of Haman's decree, intending that Haman will begin putting two and two together and start sweating profusely as a result, while Ahasuerus remains completely baffled.

If they had merely been sold into slavery, she maintains sarcastically, then of course she would never have ventured to bother His Majesty with such a trifle! What she deliberately does not say just yet is who her people are and how this threat against them has come to be made.

Ahasuerus hasn't a clue what she is talking about. But

Haman has. How he must be panicking as the realization dawns on him that all his plotting and scheming is about to rebound on his own head. Of course this is exactly what Esther wants; she wants Haman writhing in mental agony for as long as possible, while poor Ahasuerus struggles vainly to work out quite what he is missing here. We can readily imagine the colour draining from Haman's face while the king innocently enquires what his pretty little wife can possibly be referring to. For Esther has so far deliberately avoided making any express reference to Haman, just as Haman had avoided making explicit reference to the Jews. She is employing his own methods against him, giving him an acutely bitter taste of his own medicine. Just as Haman had wanted to manipulate the king into saying 'Get rid of the traitors!' before finding out who they were, so Esther now wonders if her husband will say 'Get rid of *this* traitor', before finding out who *he* is. She isn't just a pretty face after all.

Ahasuerus doesn't quite do this, but he does get very angry, before finding out who it is against whom his anger ought to be directed. He demands outright to be told what villain has issued the threat of which she speaks. 'Where is the man who has dared to do such a thing?' he fumes (Esther 7:5), thereby feeding Esther the very line she needs in order to make her triumphant announcement. And she makes it. She points calmly at Haman and says in effect, 'Look no further.'

Haman is terror-stricken. He cowers, waiting in dread to see how His Imperial Majesty will react. Rather unexpectedly, Ahasuerus walks out into the garden (7:7).

Why does he do this? It could be for any one of several reasons, or for a whole mixture of them.

1. He's so angry with Haman he's afraid he may strangle

him with his bare hands.

2. He's so angry with himself for having allowed Haman to pull the wool over his eyes for so long that he can't face either him or Esther.
3. He's in despair because yet again everything seems to be turning sour for him and he can't understand why this keeps happening.
4. He thinks that if he can get some fresh air he may be able to think more clearly and this whole confusing business will start to make sense to him.

Whatever Ahasuerus' motivation for leaving his queen and Haman alone, Haman seizes upon the opportunity to fall down before Esther and beg for her mercy. Or rather, he falls down *beside* her, on the very couch upon which she is reclining (Esther 7:8), a singularly ill-considered move, and another example of supremely bad timing on the part of this man to whom auspicious timing was all important. If we are not in touch with God, we can be spectacularly in the *wrong* place at the *wrong* time!

Perhaps Haman was still labouring under the delusion that Esther was attracted to him somehow; or perhaps he imagined that such a gracious lady couldn't possibly want to see anybody get hurt, even her deadliest foe. Either way, his pleas were no doubt falling on deaf ears, partly because Esther and Mordecai believed themselves charged with completing the task which Saul had left unfinished (as regards Agag and his descendants), and partly because Haman was just so smarmy!

But as it happens, Esther is given no opportunity to react to Haman's grovelling, because at this precise moment Ahasuerus comes back in and finds him fawning all over the queen's couch. The king exclaims (getting the wrong end of the stick as usual), 'Will he even molest the queen while she is with me in the house?'(Esther 7:8), thereby betraying once more his insecurity in his own manhood.

So straight away Haman's face gets covered again. But this time he doesn't cover it himself in shame, as he'd done after parading Mordecai round the town. This time it's the king's attendants who cover it, with a cloth, as a sign that Haman is condemned to death.

One of the eunuchs, with affected innocence, remarks at this juncture: 'A gallows seventy-five feet high stands by Haman's house. He had it made for Mordecai, who spoke up to help the king' (Esther 7:9). 'Hang him on it!' Ahasuerus roars, and this is duly done. (By the way, this is the first time in the entire story that Ahasuerus has made a real decision on his own!) Then Esther finally confesses to her royal husband that she is the cousin of Mordecai the Jew.

We aren't told how Ahasuerus takes this revelation. I don't think he can have found it particularly easy to accept. His wife has been hiding the truth from him for years, and if there was one vice which Zoroastrians abhorred above all others, it was dishonesty. Perhaps this is why Ahasuerus seems to have been so gullible: he was straight with everyone and expected them to be straight with him in return. Not only this, but having got rid of one scheming Semite, it turns out that he's married to another – and one who belongs to that particular branch of the Semitic race against whom an imperial edict has been issued. For if Ahasuerus hadn't yet succeeded in working out that the Jews and the condemned people to whom Esther was referring were one and the same, Esther must have made the fact perfectly clear to him now.

However, he must have overcome whatever scruples he had, because he proceeds to grant Esther the whole of Haman's estate. In other words, instead of Haman giving the Jews' property to the king, the king gives Haman's property to a Jew! Moreover he resolves to appoint Mordecai as his chief minister in Haman's place, presenting him with the signet ring which he'd entrusted to Haman. Perhaps he has realized that it's possible to be both shrewd and honest, and that Mordecai possesses both characteristics in full measure.

This shows that if we serve God without compromise it doesn't necessarily follow that we have to forego all worldly wealth and power. We may be *given* it (compare the story of Joseph in Egypt), but we must not seek it for ourselves, nor for its own end. We must seek God only, and accept whatever circumstances he sends us. But it is a biblical principle that if we show ourselves faithful with a little responsibility, we shall be given more. It also shows that power needn't corrupt if we stay close to God. You can be loyal to both temporal and eternal authority, to the king and to God, though sometimes conflict may arise.

The fall of Haman has now been perfectly balanced by the rise of the man he sought to destroy. Although all this seems like a fitting end to the saga, we still haven't reached the point where everyone lives happily ever after. There is a very important loose end remaining to be tied; in fact it's an end *so* loose that if it *isn't* tied, triumph will turn rapidly back into tragedy. For Haman's execution has achieved nothing so far as the fate of the Jewish race is concerned. As we have carefully been told, the law of the Medes and the Persians cannot be changed, so the edict against the Jews still stands.

Not only is the story not over, but its most controversial section is yet to come . . .

13

The Jews Fight Back

It was some while before the truth dawned on Queen Esther that the lives of her people the Jews were still on the line. In her moment of triumph, as she watched Haman being led away to die, the excitement that welled up inside her caused her to forget temporarily that no edict of the Persian king could ever be revoked.

Briefly it seemed to her that everything was right with the world once more; she had regained her husband's favour, and as their eyes met across the empty dishes on the table, nothing else at all seemed to matter. They were alone together at last, and when Ahasuerus again moved up close to take her in his arms, she did not try to pull away. He was so handsome, so virile, with his lithe huntsman's physique, his sleekly curled hair tumbling over broad, muscular shoulders . . . and in spite of his numerous faults and failings, Esther was in love with him still. As his lips covered hers, she kissed him in return; as he folded her beneath him on the couch she put her arms about his neck, for she was as sick with desire for him as he was for her.

It was only the following day, when he had got up to attend to affairs of state and she lay by herself on her bed in the morning sunshine, that the truth came home to her. She might be back in the king's good books, and Mordecai might be wearing Haman's shoes – perhaps as individuals the two of them no longer had any reason to live in dread of the future. But nothing had been said at any stage which would alter the sorry fate of the rest of their people.

At first Esther rolled over on her pillows and told herself not to worry. Mordecai was First Minister now; he would see to it that everything turned out all right.

Yet what if he was not able to? What if he had tried already and been told there was nothing that could be done? Esther heaved a sigh of resignation. For she recognized that she would have to broach the subject with Ahasuerus once again, and once again risk provoking his wrath by pleading the Jewish cause.

Not that this decision came to her easily. There was a pernicious little voice inside her head that was insistently telling her to leave well alone. It had been one thing to go before the king when she'd been out of his favour, this voice argued; in a way she'd had little to lose. But now that she had regained Ahasuerus' love and respect, surely it would be sheer foolishness for her to risk losing them all over again.

Yet Esther knew full well that this voice was not the voice of God. Although she was faced with a fresh dilemma, there could be no shadow of a doubt this time as to what God was expecting her to do. And just as she had sensed his presence with her when she had approached the king before, so she was confident that he would go with her again, and that somehow the impossible could be achieved. The only real question that Esther had to answer was when and where would be the appropriate time and place for her to make her new appeal? Should she wait until the evening, when once again she was alone with Ahasuerus in informal privacy? She had already learned the value of patience, and had seen it work successfully to her advantage.

But something told her that this time there was nothing to

be gained from waiting. Indeed, much might be lost, if she were to allow their marital intimacy, so recently restored, to be soured by her introducing politics into the bedroom. So she resolved to go at once and request a formal audience with the king in the Apadana, where she would lay her burden publicly before him.

And this is exactly what she did. Since there was no longer any reason why she should not be granted permission to enter, she was admitted without demur to the royal presence, where she fell on the ground at her husband's feet. There, suddenly unable to hold back the tears, she gave herself up to grief for her stricken people.

*   *   *

Actually, the author doesn't tell us in so many words where this scene takes place. For in setting it in the Apadana I admit to having read between his lines. A cursory reading of his account could well lead us to imagine that the scene follows on immediately from the one before, and that Esther and her husband were still lingering over the meal they had shared with Haman when she put her case to him. But we're told that she threw herself down at Ahasuerus' feet in order to beg him to issue a second edict to countermand the first one, and that when she did so, he held out the sceptre once again to indicate that she should arise and address him standing. This only makes sense in a formal context. He wouldn't have sat clutching his sceptre at the dinner table!

Prostrate at her husband's feet and wetting them with her tears, Esther was no longer acting the part of the cool sophisticate. Something in the language of the passage (Esther 8:3–4) convinces us that at last we are seeing her true feelings. We're reminded of the heart-rending scene in Genesis 45 when Joseph, as prime minister of Egypt, having led his long-lost brothers a merry dance, can no longer mask his emotions and breaks down weeping before them.

Ahasuerus bids his wife get up from the floor, and she does so, collecting herself together enough to present a reasoned case. 'Your Majesty,' she says, 'if you truly care about me, and about justice, please issue a proclamation to prevent Haman's orders being carried out. He was a son of Agag – an Amalekite. That's why he wanted to destroy all the Jews in your empire.' But she sums up by giving way to her emotions once more and sobbing, 'How can I bear to see disaster fall on my people? How can I bear to witness the destruction of my own flesh and blood?' (Esther 8:6).

At first it appears that her tears have been cried in vain. Ahasuerus seems to be saying that he's already done all he can: he has had Haman hanged, and given Esther his property. An edict issued in the king's name and stamped with the royal seal simply cannot be revoked.

But then a loophole in the law is found. Ahasuerus announces that Esther and Mordecai may publish another decree in the king's name, so long as it does not directly contradict the first one.

How bizarre this seems to us, and it must have seemed equally bizarre to Esther and Mordecai. Throughout the book the bizarre, unnatural order of Persian life has been in constant tension with the clear moral outlook of Mordecai, the laws of whose people, it is implied, come from a higher, unquestionable authority. We are meant to grasp that almost everything about the Jewish exiles' host nation is unnatural – its laws, its sexuality, its extravagant materialism.

The royal secretaries gather once more, and this time the letter they send to the satraps and governors is at Mordecai's dictation. The wording of Esther 8:9 is deliberately identical to that of 3:12, showing how the tables have now been turned. Now the *Jews* are to 'destroy, kill, annihilate'.

What we learn of the letter's content demonstrates both the author's familiarity with Persia and the creative sharpness of Mordecai's thought. He recognizes that on the appointed day no one will be able to prevent the Jews from being attacked by those who hate them because imperial authorization for the attack has been given. But they can be given permission to organize and arm themselves in self-defence.

So the irrevocability of Persian law ends up empowering the Jews! If the slaughter had simply been called off, Haman's sons and the rest of the Jews' enemies would have lived on and continued to spread their poisonous lies about God's people. As it is, they were to be destroyed as a result of the Jews rising up in self-defence.

Couriers are despatched at top speed to take the letters, on special fast horses (Esther 8:14). Super-express delivery is required to disseminate the good news! Jubilant rejoicing breaks out among the Jews of Shushan, and subsequently throughout the empire, as if they have defeated their enemies already, though in fact everyone still has to wait nine months before Haman's 'auspicious day' arrives. (Three months seem to have been lost along the way somewhere, in that when the original edict was issued there was almost a year to go until the dread day arrived. Perhaps it was actually *three months* before the truth dawned on Esther and Mordecai that their people were still under threat.)

Imagine having to sit tight for nine months knowing that you were going to have to fight for your very life and the lives of your loved ones on a predetermined day. What phenomenal patience must have been required! I don't suppose that many of us are ever likely to find ourselves in remotely similar circumstances. Yet similar patience can be required of us in other contexts. God doesn't always answer our prayers straight away, and the more serious the thing we are praying about, the longer it can seem to take before an answer is forthcoming. Sometimes we have to be patient for months or even years for 'all things to work together for good'.

Why can't God answer us more quickly? Surely he who was able to create the universe out of nothing, and who will be able to change us into his Son's imperishable likeness in 'the twinkling of an eye' (1 Corinthians 15:52) when he comes again, could answer our most fervent prayers instantaneously, if he really loved us.

There are several reasons why he does not always answer instantly. One is the principle of free will: God will not force anyone's hand. For example, if we are praying for the salvation of friends or relatives, we have to wait while God gently draws them to himself through the ponderings of their hearts and minds or the events of their lives. Another reason is something we have mentioned before: God is actually much more interested in moulding our characters than he is in changing our circumstances. Patience is a fruit of the Spirit, and we cannot develop it unless there are things for us to be patient about!

The general jubilation in response to Mordecai's letter is equal and opposite to the consternation that had broken out throughout the whole population when the original edict was issued. Another of the story's great ironic reversals takes place at this juncture. There must have been many Jews who had hoped to escape being identified as such when the edict against them came out. But now many non-Jews suddenly profess that they are Jewish (Esther 8:17)! Perhaps some were genuinely converted to belief in the Jewish God as a result of witnessing what they couldn't help but interpret as divine intervention on the Jews' behalf. But there may have been others more cynical who realized that with Mordecai's spectacular promotion their bread was now buttered on the other side.

This is in fact the only reference to Gentiles becoming Jews in the whole of the Old Testament, though the New Testament bears ample witness to the practice in the first century AD (Matthew 23:15; Acts 2:11, etc.).

At long last the fateful day arrives and the famous bloodbath to which I referred in my Introduction ensues. Instead of the Jews being wiped out by their enemies, the very opposite happens.

So, were Mordecai and Esther acting rightly in sanctioning all this killing? Many commentators have thought not, but I strongly disagree. Most of their objections seem to stem from the fact that they reckon the Jews massacred innocent women and children as well as men, since this was what had been going to happen to their women and children.

But the text doesn't need to be taken this way at all. The Jews' action was purely defensive, and targeted only at those who came actively against *them* and *their* women and children. It is unlikely that imperial troops were involved, on either side. The text implies that the Jews were given a free hand without imperial interference. It says: 'They did as they pleased to those who hated them' (Esther 9:5). The Jews' struggle was only against the proto-Nazis who wanted them annihilated; the great majority of Persians either kept well out of it, or else actually assisted the Jewish cause, because a Jew now occupied the highest office in the government. The Jews did not massacre any innocent people whatsoever.

If one believes that violence is always wrong, even when used in self-defence, then Esther and Mordecai did act wrongly. But unfortunately for those who hold such a view, the Bible is not a pacifist book. It recognizes that there can be circumstances in which the use of violence is justified –

indeed, when it would be wrong not to use it. Even in the
New Testament, when Roman soldiers come to John the
Baptist and ask how they should live, he doesn't tell them
to leave the army, but merely to be content with their pay
and not extort money from others (Luke 3:14). Nor does
Jesus tell the officer whose servant he heals (Luke 7:1–10)
that he ought to consider a change of career.

We learn from Esther 9:7 that the ten sons of Haman have
all been killed in the fighting. Of course, this is highly
significant. It means that Agag's line is cut off at last!
Amalek is finished! Never again will the Jews be threatened
by sons of Amalek who ought never to have existed. Agag
himself must already have had children when Samuel killed
him, otherwise his line would already have been extinct;
Esther wanted to ensure that there were none of his
descendants left this time around, lest the race survive after
all. For at last the command given in Deuteronomy 25:19
has been taken seriously: 'You shall blot out the memory of
Amalek from under heaven. Do not forget!' It is probably
this command that gave rise to the custom of children
blotting out the name of Haman with football rattles during
the reading of the Esther scroll at the festival of Purim. Just
as the verse from Deuteronomy contains a paradox (blot out
the memory/do not forget!), so the custom is paradoxical
too: you have to listen out for Haman's name so that you
can proceed to drown it! And what tremendous fun this
must be. When it comes to customs calculated to appeal to
children, Judaism really has it sussed.

However, we are also told in the same passage (Esther
9:7–10) that the Jews didn't take any plunder, in spite of
the fact that permission had been granted them to do so.
Altogether the text stresses this three times (see also 9:15
and 16). I think this is another reference to the story of Saul;
in addition to sparing Agag, whom he should have killed,

Saul had taken plunder which he should have destroyed. Esther and Mordecai must systematically undo each of his mistakes. Besides, the refusal to take plunder, in a world where plundering was seen as the automatic right of the victor, would have made a memorable impact on those who heard about it.

But at the end of the day, Esther is not satisfied. She wants a second day of slaughter, and also to have the bodies of Haman's sons hanged on gallows. And so the commentators' objections come flooding in again thick and fast. Surely one day of slaughter is enough for anyone? And why hang men who are already dead? Isn't this plain vindictiveness?

Again, I say they are wrong. The slaughter had to continue because some of the Jews' enemies in Shushan were still alive. It may be that the slaughter on the first day had taken place in the citadel/acropolis only, not in the rest of Shushan. (This may be the meaning of Esther 9:11.) And presumably there were more enemies of the Jews per capita in Shushan than anywhere else because Haman's propaganda would have been most effective closest to home. If they had been allowed to live, their menace would have continued to exist, they would have spread their anti-Semitic lies and within days, weeks or months the Jews would have had just as many enemies as before. Opposition which is not quelled always festers and grows. Perhaps in the long run millions of lives were saved! We can't tell, nor, as we have already noted, should we judge God by human standards. (If Joshua had done as he was told and wiped out all the Canaanites, it's almost certain that in the long run *less* blood would have been shed.)

As for Haman's sons, it was fitting that their bodies should end up on public display, because this is what had happened to Saul and *his* sons. Saul's mission was at last complete, Amalek was no more, and in a sense Saul himself was now avenged.

But how can all this talk of slaughter and revenge have any meaningful application for Christians living in the twenty-first century? Certainly it must make us feel rather uncomfortable to say the least, when much of the *non-*Christian world seems to have progressed beyond this sort of thing, and would regard the content of 'Esther's' later chapters as the epitome of political incorrectness, not to say primitive tribal barbarism. In an age when even governments can talk positively about reconciliation, and contemplate the cancellation of Third World debt, isn't it rather embarrassing for us as Christians to be saddled with a Bible that is deeply stained with blood, much of it shed at God's express command?

I think we have to admit that in this area there is a distinct difference between the Old Testament and the New. To use the example quoted by Jesus himself, Moses in the Old Testament endorses 'an eye for an eye and a tooth for a tooth' (Exodus 21:24) whereas Jesus tells us to 'turn the other cheek' (Matthew 5:38–39). I am not saying that the New Testament roundly condemns war of any kind, because I have already shown that it does not; but it does make clear that there is no place for vindictiveness in the life of a Christian. (See, for example, Romans 12:18–21.)

Yet this very obvious difference between the Old and New Testaments should not cause us to become perplexed. It is not that God has changed in some way over the centuries. The point is that he has had to educate his people gradually; it would not have been appropriate for him to bestow the new covenant in all its fullness upon a primitive, tribal people who had scarcely emerged from slavery and rank idolatry. Undoubtedly in the Bible we can trace an educative process; Paul himself calls the Old Testament law 'a schoolmaster to bring us to Christ' (Galatians 3:24, AV) and explains in Galatians 4:1–5 that the Jews had had a lot of learning to do before it was the right time for Christ to come into the world. Therefore it would be quite wrong for us to conclude that every passage of the Bible can and should be applied indiscriminately to our lives today. Some of God's commands were given for very specific occasions and very specific reasons, and when we read the Scriptures we must do so with intelligence and under the guidance of the Holy Spirit. 'Esther' has a great deal to say to us about what life was like for the Jews living in a particular place and at a particular time, and it also undoubtedly contains principles which are of a universal significance; for instance, the necessity for us as God's people to be willing to stick our own necks out and jeopardize our own physical well-being in order to stand up for those who are unjustly threatened or oppressed.

But this does not mean that we should go about plotting revenge on those who hate us. Jesus categorically told us to love our enemies and pray for those who persecute us (Matthew 5:44). As Jesus explains to his disciples in Mark 10:5, Moses' law made allowances for the fact that his people were so hard-hearted, but now that we have beheld God incarnate in the world, and have received his Spirit to renew us, the old ways are no longer good enough. Jesus himself provides us with the supreme example of this development: rather than killing his enemies, he allowed them to kill him. And yet through his resurrection he conquered the ultimate enemy, death, more comprehensively than any earthly general has ever conquered his mortal foe.

Likewise, we as Christians ought to think very carefully about how we relate to those in the world today whose ethics are still based substantially on the Old Testament rather than the New. I refer specifically to the Jews, and above all to the struggle of many of them against the Palestinian Arabs for possession of the Holy Land. While there are of course Jews living in the State of Israel who see the pressing need for these two proud peoples to be reconciled, and for the establishment of peaceful co-existence, there are others who would still regard sections of the Old Testament, including the final chapters of 'Esther', as a mandate for them to slaughter all their enemies today. There are some Christians who seem to assume that it is automatically right to make common cause with Zionists/Orthodox Jewish settlers on the West Bank, etc., because God originally promised them the land.

But things are no longer so simple. Yes, there are Old Testament prophecies which may mean that the Jews will return to their land before Jesus comes again, but actually we aren't told whether this is a good thing or not. It's just like saying that before the end comes there will be famines, earthquakes, wars and rumours of wars (see Matthew 24:6–7). So there will, but we aren't supposed to welcome them, and still less to start them!

During our first visit to Israel, Keith and I met a delightful Palestinian family living on the slopes of the hill at Gibeah, when we were searching for the site of Saul's fortress. Jewish high-rise developments were encroaching on them by the day. If their home hasn't already been buried beneath yet another Jerusalem suburb, it very soon will be, despite the fact that their ancestors had owned and farmed that piece of land for centuries, and the setting was beautiful.

The travel writer William Dalrymple[1] tells of having met Palestinian families, the ruins of whose homes were passed off by Jewish tour guides as Roman remains! These people

---

1. William Dalrymple, *From the Holy Mountain* (HarperCollins, 1997).

had been driven from their village by force, and had then had to watch the bulldozers move in to flatten their little houses. A well which the guides claimed had been dug in antiquity had actually been dug by an old man Dalrymple met: he'd dug it as a boy, with his father. Perhaps some of those Christians who side so enthusiastically with the Jews should go and visit Israel and talk to Palestinians themselves.

14

Happily Ever After?

Just as we don't know very much at all about Esther before she was taken to live at the palace, so we have no idea what became of her once the fateful conflict was over. All we do know about is the institution of the Purim festival (Esther 9:18–32), which some hostile commentators reckon to be the sole reason for the book of Esther's existence.

We are told that Mordecai and Esther both wrote letters to all the Jews in the empire instructing them to observe the 14th and 15th of Adar as days of joy and feasting every year. The massacre had happened on the 13th and 14th, so it's not the massacre that is being celebrated, but its end. Incidentally, it's Esther who has the last word on the subject. Her letter goes out after her cousin's, giving his words her queenly seal of approval.

So Haman's plan to destroy the Jews actually resulted in a festival which has helped unite and sustain them as a people over the centuries. So much for Haman's lucky day: he didn't even live to see it!

Today Purim is one of the most joyful observances of Judaism, although Jews have not always agreed among themselves as to its relative importance. Some reckon it a minor festival on account of the fact that it is not mentioned in the Torah, the most sacred collection of Jewish scriptures.

But many rabbis have claimed that its observance *is* authorized by the Torah, because Haman was an Amalekite and Exodus 17:14 looks forward to the Amalekites' total destruction.

Most of the Purim celebrations still take place on the 14th of Adar (in February/March), after a day spent fasting to commemorate Esther's own fast. In every synagogue the book of Esther is read out from a special handwritten parchment. Rattles, drums, whistles and even dustbin lids are used to drown out Haman's name whenever it is read, and there is a great deal of shouting and booing and cheering where appropriate. Children perform plays telling Esther's story, and sing Purim songs, and three-cornered pastries filled with poppy seeds are eaten, called 'Haman's ears', or 'Haman's pockets'.

The next day is called Shushan Purim, commemorating the fact that the Jews of Shushan didn't overcome all their enemies until the following day. In some of Israel's most ancient cities Purim itself is kept on the 15th of Adar, not the 14th.

During the festival period, gifts are exchanged and alms are given to the poor. In Israel, streets are decorated with flags and buntings, and there are processions through the major cities. Masquerading parties carouse through the night, because drunkenness is actively encouraged, being accorded the status of a 'mitzvah' (a sort of obligatory 'good deed') at this one special time of year. As you'll probably recall from the Introduction, if you're taking part in the Purim festivities you're supposed to drink and keep on drinking until you can't distinguish Haman's name from Mordecai's.

I must say that this encouragement of drunkenness does not come from the book of Esther itself: the Bible's position on drunkenness is that it is always to be avoided. (There is a hilarious passage on the evil effects of drunkenness in

Proverbs 23:29–35.) As we have already noted (see Chapter 3), it isn't that there's anything wrong with alcohol in its own right, or in the drinking of it in moderate amounts (though some people are wise to avoid it altogether if they feel they need to). It's that an excess of alcohol impairs judgement and self-control. Anything which impairs our judgement and self-control is to be avoided by those who live to please God.

The Jews themselves argue about where the custom of Purim drunkenness comes from. Some say it originated because the Jews found their salvation in the drinking feasts Esther threw for Ahasuerus and Haman; others emphasize the more mystical dimension of transcending the everyday distinctions between good and evil.

Another Purim custom which is forbidden to Jews at other times of the year is that of men dressing up as women and vice versa. Deuteronomy 22:5 expressly forbids cross-dressing in normal circumstances, but at Purim Jews permit it. Also at Purim, students are allowed to lampoon their teachers, and invent absurd interpretations of Jewish teaching. All these arguably irreverent customs are representative of the type of topsy-turvy behaviour associated with Saturnalia or the Feast of Fools, many of which live on in our tradition of the pantomime – and frequently cause offence!

So much for the importance of Purim in the religious calendar of the Jews. But can it have any relevance for Christians in the modern world? Certainly Christians have never paid much attention to the Purim festival as such, probably because, unlike some of the other Jewish festivals, it played no significant part in the earthly life of Jesus as the Gospel writers have recorded it. Therefore it was not taken up by the church and 'Christianized', as were Passover and Pentecost for example. It is impossible for us to celebrate Easter without thinking back to Passover, because Jesus has been cast in the role of Passover lamb, sacrificed to pay for his people's sins. Likewise the Christian festival of Whitsun, which celebrates the coming of the Holy Spirit, is inextricably bound up with the Jewish festival of Pentecost which was being celebrated at the time. Purim, on the other hand, seems uncompromisingly Jewish, of relevance only to the members of that indomitable though frequently per- secuted race.

However, even though we as Christians may not have adopted Purim as a festival, we have every good reason to celebrate the survival of the Jews as a people, not merely for their own sake but for ours. I am reminded of Revelation 12:1–6 and 13–17, which depicts God's people, the Jews, as a woman about to give birth who is threatened by a vicious dragon. It was a Jewish woman who was to give birth to the Messiah, Jesus Christ, and had the dragon been allowed to devour Mary's ancestors in the time of Esther, God's plan of salvation might have come to nothing. Over and over again in the Old Testament the dragon almost succeeded: for example, at the time of the famine, when the sons of Jacob would have perished from starvation had not their brother Joseph risen to a position of influence in Egypt; during the exodus when Pharaoh's charioteers would have caught the Jews and butchered them all had not the waters of the Red Sea returned to their place and swallowed them; when Jerusalem so nearly fell to the Assyrians, and then did fall to the Babylonians. Yet through it all a remnant was preserved, and from that remnant Jesus emerged just as God had always intended that he would do. On each of the occasions when the Chosen People were threatened, their survival depended on God's active intervention, thus demonstrating that however the powers of darkness seek to thwart him, God's sovereignty will prevail in the end.

But what of Esther herself? Did she and Ahasuerus succeed in living happily ever after as husband and wife at last? The Bible does not tell us, but if the extra-biblical accounts are to be believed, then they did not. Herodotus expressly tells us that Xerxes was outlived by Amestris (Vashti) to whom he was certainly married at the time of his death – much to the latter's chagrin.

In any case, personally I find it hard to imagine that Esther and Ahasuerus could have succeeded in building a stable, lasting union. They were too different, and the crisis through which they had come must have served only to accentuate these differences.

Not only did they belong to two different religions, but Esther had shown herself to be a remarkably intelligent and resourceful individual, while Ahasuerus had emerged as something of a dupe. Even at the end of the story he's still getting the wrong end of the stick, imagining that Haman is trying to rape his wife when in fact he's begging her for his life. Ahasuerus was a victim of his own exalted status, hemmed in by protocol and legal restrictions; although in a supremely powerful position, he was not a powerful person in himself. Until challenged directly by Esther he had been perfectly prepared to sit by and watch the Jews massacred to a man, simply because a decree had gone out to that effect and it hadn't occurred to him to think up an alternative.

Surely such a feeble-minded creature would not have satisfied a capable, full-blooded woman like Esther? I'm in no doubt that she *did* find him enormously attractive, physically speaking, but a handsome face and honed muscles weren't going to be enough to sustain her interest in the long run. Sexual passion was one thing; mutual compatibility was something else, and any steps the couple may have tried to take in order to build their relationship into something deeper are likely to have come up against insurmountable barriers every time. Ahasuerus wasn't much of a Prince Charming, in actual fact; and besides, would he have been happy to eat kosher food?

So, in the absence of facts, let's indulge in a little romantic fantasy! (I'm a novelist at heart, after all.) I think that after the Jews were saved, Esther went back to her life of obscurity. She knew that Ahasuerus was still deeply in love with Vashti; and if a way had been found to save the Jews in spite of the royal edict against them, then surely a way could be found to restore Vashti too. For example, the terms of her banishment could have been reinterpreted to mean that she was merely prohibited from appearing ever again before the king *officially* – in other words, when he was seated on his throne. Perhaps Esther herself suggested this reinterpretation, and worked for her predecessor's reinstatement.

If this is what happened, it would enable us to reconcile the biblical account with that of Herodotus, in which Xerxes/Ahasuerus and Amestris/Vashti are still together at the time of the former's death in 465 BC (in which it's likely that the latter had quite a part to play . . .).

Perhaps Esther married again, in an effort to preserve the Saulides from extinction, but if she did, there is no record of her having succeeded in her aim. So far as we know, Saul's line died with her, just as surely as Agag's did, and doubtless this was as it was meant to be. Saul had lost the throne of Israel through his disobedience in not putting Agag to death, and no Saulide was ever supposed to sit on it again.

Maybe Esther knew all this. Maybe she *didn't* marry again. Maybe she just went back to keeping house for Mordecai – which had been the height of her ambition during her blackest moments when cooped up with her jealous rivals in Hegai's virgins' harem.

Or maybe she didn't. I like to think that when she said goodbye and good riddance to her life as Persian queen, there was one person left behind whom she suddenly realized she didn't want to forget. Hegai himself, who had once befriended her and shown her favour; Hegai, who had helped fashion for her the image which would lead to her being chosen as queen in the first place; Hegai, for whom she had scarcely spared a thought since the day she'd passed from his care, but who had thought of little else but her in all those years. He had remained in the king's employ, looking after the hapless virgins who had never got to spend a night with the king but whose parents could not find them dowries and refused to take them back. But he was in a job without a future; like the women in his care, he had nothing to look forward to except old age and death.

So when one day out of the blue he received a letter from Esther informing him that she had made arrangements for him to leave the palace and work for her, he gave a whoop of delight, and his fellow eunuchs couldn't see him for dust. He set up home with the only person who had ever valued his friendship, and together they devoted their lives to looking after Jewish children who had been orphaned in the two-day conflict. After all, both of them knew what it was like to be an orphan. And in a sense *every* Jewish child belonged to Esther. They might all have been dead without her.

Conclusions

Our survey of the book of Esther is complete! But before closing the curtains once more upon its colourful if violent world, I'd like to return briefly to the questions posed in the Introduction, to see whether we have answered them satisfactorily. Or, if we have not yet answered them in so many words, whether we are now in a position to do so. We asked ourselves whether the events described in the book ever really happened; whether Esther and Mordecai acted rightly in baying for their enemies' blood; why God is so conspicious by his absence throughout the narrative; and why the book was named after Esther and not after Mordecai.

While we are in the process of answering these questions, I'd like to address some new ones, too. What, if anything, have we learned about God? What have we learned about Esther and her achievement, and about ourselves?

First of all, can we accept that the events of the book represent a real episode in history, or not? At its very beginning we find the Hebrew word *wayehi*, which means 'Now it came to pass . . .'. This is a deliberate use of the formula with which historical sections of the Bible begin (see for example 1 Kings 6:1). And at the end we find the following: 'All his [Ahasuerus'] acts of power and might,

together with a full account of the greatness of Mordecai . . .
are they not written in the book of the annals of the kings of
Media and Persia?' (Esther 10:2). This is exactly the
formula with which the reign of each of the kings of Israel
and Judah ends in the books of Kings (see 1 Kings 22:39:
'As for the other events of Ahab's reign . . . are they not
written in the book of the annals of the kings of Israel?').
Incidentally, none of these annals survives, so far as we
know, which is a great pity. As a historical novelist, I'd
really love to get my hands on them!

It seems to me that by using the biblical formulae in this
way, the author of 'Esther' is telling us one of two things:
either that his book is just as authentically historical as
Kings or that it's satire after all – in other words, he's using
the formulae sarcastically, and the book is framed by his
mischievous little jokes.

But as we have seen, there is no reason to suppose that
the events of the book could not have happened exactly as
described. The author is careful to give us details as to the
time and place of each piece of action, dating it all
according to the regnal years of the Persian king. He doesn't
just say 'Once upon a time' or something of the kind. He
demonstrates an exceedingly accurate knowledge of Persian
life and customs, and the events he describes have precisely
the same ring to them as passages about Persia in
Herodotus. Granted, Herodotus was a storyteller as much as
he was a historian, but since we don't have 'the book of the
annals of the kings of Media and Persia', or any such
Persian writings, he's just about the best source we have to
go on.

It seems to me highly significant that the first-century
Jewish writer Josephus, who was much better qualified than
we are to judge the genre of a piece of ancient Jewish
literature and to spot Hebrew sarcasm when he saw it,

incorporates the events of 'Esther' quite naturally into his history of the Israelite nation. No one seems to have told *him* that it was just a novel.

It strikes me that attempts to deny the historicity of 'Esther' are disturbingly similar to neo-Nazi attempts to deny that the holocaust ever happened. It seems astonishing that anyone could doubt the reality of Hitler's appalling atrocities, when we have so many metres of newsreel and so many photographs of the emaciated corpses that were bulldozed into mass graves. But some Jews fear that when the last of the survivors are dead, people will begin to believe the neo-Nazis' claims, simply because they will assume that a thing so dreadful could never have happened in our civilized era, that it must have been exaggerated out of all proportion, and that the photos and newsreel are documenting just one or two isolated incidents. If people don't want to believe that something happened, then they won't, however strong the evidence.

Certain aspects of the book of Esther *are* a little disturbing to modern readers, Christians included. Esther doesn't exactly 'do good to her enemies' by any stretch of the imagination, and a great deal of blood flows at her instigation. But I think we have found convincing answers to such objections. Esther wasn't living in our century; her world was not yet ready for the revolutionary teachings of Jesus, and the very survival of her people was at stake.

And of course, the fact that the Jewish race survived down to the beginning of the Christian era is just as important to Christians as it is to Jews, since it was from the Jewish people that the Messiah was to arise. As we have already observed, if the Jews had been comprehensively wiped out, what would have become of God's strategy for redemption? As I mentioned at the beginning of this study, while Ruth was an ancestor of Jesus, Esther may well have had no children at all. However, were it not for what Esther achieved, Ruth's line might have been cut off and there might have been no home for Jesus to be born into.We might have had to wait many more centuries for the incarnation of Christ if God had had to begin the preparations for his coming all over again.

So why doesn't the book mention God? I think we have answered this question too. The author was writing for an audience that had much in common with the society in which we live today: it was multicultural, cosmopolitan, sophisticated. He knew that many of his potential readers – secularized Jews as well as Persians – would be reluctant to read a pious tome full of religious jargon. So he crafted something eminently readable, but in which the hand of God was clearly at work.

I'm reminded of a colleague I used to teach with who, although Jewish herself, innocently asked me 'And who's Esther?' when I told her what I was writing about! 'Only the most famous heroine in your people's history!' I had to tell her. I would guess that many of the Jews of ancient Persia were as assimilated into non-Jewish culture as she was.

Basically, I think that our author wrote his book in the way that he did for exactly the same reason as I write my novels. Like him, I want to introduce people to the world of faith in as painless and entertaining a way as possible, while at the same time stimulating them to think for themselves about spiritual things.

He was probably also writing to show that there could be a legitimate reason for some Jews not having returned to Israel. God might have providentially placed them where they were for a purpose, to defend the existence of the community which *had* returned. His book was written as an affirmation that God was still with his people even when they were in exile, and even when his name wasn't being bandied about all the time. He was just as powerful outside the borders of the land of Israel as he was inside; diaspora Jewish communities did have a future, as it was possible to be simultaneously loyal to God and to a Gentile king.

It seems to me that in this respect 'Esther' is one of the most relevant books in the whole of the Bible, to those of us living in a post-Christian culture. It assumes no previous knowledge of religion, and doesn't ram it down anyone's throat. It isn't laced with spectacular miraculous events which might put off a non-religious reader by leading him to suppose that 'faith is believing things you know aren't true'. Nor is it full of references to God 'speaking' to people, as though his voice were as easy to hear as your mother's when she's calling you to dinner. It's written for people like us, or like our non-Christian friends, and the events it describes have the ring of truth to them.

Yes, there are several startling coincidences involved, but they are exactly the kind of coincidences that do happen in real life, and which ought to convince us that there is a benevolent intelligence behind our universe, even though others may just put them down to 'luck'. Few of us hear God's voice audibly; few of us have performed spectacular miracles; but we have all faced dilemmas in which in our heart of hearts we knew exactly what God wanted us to do, and we can all look back across the years and see ways in which we have been guided. In 'Esther' God is literally conspicuous by his absence – his influence is over-whelmingly conspicuous all the way through! In spite of Haman's strenuous efforts to destroy them, God's people survive and flourish, because God protects them – though he does not always act in accordance with their expectations. But ultimately God is sovereign; his purposes cannot be thwarted. And the unseen hand which shaped events in ancient Shushan is no less active in our world today.

So, what is the book of Esther trying to teach us about this omnipresent God and about how we should live as his people?

Firstly, I think it tells us very clearly that he cares passionately for us, and that he can and does intervene on our behalf to prevent wicked men ill-treating us against his will. This is not to say that we will never suffer, or that life will always jog along happily in the direction we think it should go. But provided that we maintain close fellowship with God and listen attentively to the prompting of his Holy Spirit in our hearts, things will never get beyond his control.

Secondly, I think it's telling us that assimilation and persecution are two equal, if opposite, dangers. Living as Christians in a largely tolerant society presents us with its own challenges; very often it's harder for us to make an impact on our neighbours than it is for our brothers and sisters who have to live under oppressive political regimes or among militant members of other faiths. What better way to ensure that the church grows among teenagers than by making it illegal for anyone under eighteen to attend! Yet this used to be the law in many Communist countries.

Thirdly, 'Esther' teaches us that we are not to live our lives according to the principles of fate or luck. True happiness does not depend upon winning the lottery, nor upon planetary conjunctions. Reading our horoscopes in the daily paper is not a harmless bit of fun; it is the Enemy's way of keeping us in bondage to our birth and background, when God has so much more in store for each and every one of us. Faith enables us to rise above what fate may have in store, and seek our destiny. If only we will cut the cords that tie us to the ground, we shall indeed 'mount up with wings as eagles' (Isaiah 40:31) and be spiritually free.

Fourthly, although God is unquestionably sovereign, we, like Esther, are sometimes called upon to take the initiative.

It is not that God *needs* us to do his work for him; rather, as a loving parent, he *chooses* to work with us his children, to *involve* us in what he is doing, so that we may share in his joy when we see his plans come to fruition. Taking an active part in God's work is a tremendous responsibility, but a tremendous privilege too – and of course, he never leaves us to shoulder the responsibility alone. Just as Esther knew the presence of God close beside her when she risked her life to go before the Persian king upon his throne, so we too can move forward confident in the knowledge that God goes with us.

It's true that sometimes God seems silent and his people powerless; and it is at times like this that we may be tempted to go it alone and do what *we* think ought to be done. But taking the initiative at God's instigation – a good thing – is not the same as deciding what God ought to be doing, and doing that – a very bad thing, which leads nowhere except to frustration and failure. If we keep our spiritual eyes and ears open we shall be able to discern what God is doing and what our part in it should be. Even Jesus said: 'The Son can do nothing by himself; he can only do what he sees his Father doing' (John 5:19).

We have still left one of our original questions unanswered, and it is to this remaining question that I should like to turn in closing. Why is the book we have been studying called the book of Esther, and not the book of Mordecai?

Partly it's because Esther does indeed emerge as initiator of the most important sequences of action, and because she does get the last word, sending out her own letter about Purim to lend weight to Mordecai's.

But also I think it's because the book is predominantly about her, about how she went from being a pretty young thing with no sense of responsibility towards her people and no real faith, to being a complete, fulfilled human being with genuine strength of character.

Mordecai's life was changed too, of course: he rose from obscurity to a position of phenomenal power, proving thereby that integrity isn't necessarily an obstacle to getting on in the world. Nor is it impossible to hold high office without compromising one's principles.

But the changes in Mordecai's circumstances were essentially material, while Esther also changed spiritually. Her life was dramatically changed as a result of an encounter with God, in which she was made to face up to who he was and who she was, and how there was meant to be a real relationship between them. We all need to encounter God in this pivotal way.

In other words, just as Esther came to be Queen of Persia 'for such a time as this', so her book has a great deal to say to us in our day too. Indeed, I believe that we ourselves live in precisely the sort of times for which it was written.

Index of Life Issues

Mary: The Mother of Jesus

by Wendy Virgo

MARY is the prototype Christian woman. No illusions about herself, no expectations of being 'special'. But ready to do God's will, however strange or inconvenient or costly that may be.

From the first Christmas to the first Easter and beyond, we follow Mary, the mother of Jesus. Wendy Virgo's skilful and moving narrative brings to life the dilemmas and dangers, the pride and the pain, of being the mother of the most special Person in history.

WENDY VIRGO has been married to New Frontiers International leader Terry since 1968 and they have five children. She has run seminars for leaders' wives and been a speaker at various women's gatherings.

K Kingsway Publications